THE ONE-PAGE PROPOSAL

HOW TO GET YOUR BUSINESS PITCH ONTO ONE PERSUASIVE PAGE

PATRICK G. RILEY

ReganBooks

An Imprint of HarperCollins*Publishers*

HarperCollins books may be purchased for educational, business, or sales promotional use. For information please write: Special Markets Department, HarperCollins Publishers Inc., 10 East 53rd Street, New York, NY 10022.

FIRST EDITION

Designed by Nancy Singer Olaguera

Library of Congress Cataloging-in-Publication Data
Riley, Patrick G.
    The one-page proposal: how to get your business pitch onto one persuasive page /
  Patrick G. Riley.
      p.   cm.
    ISBN 0-06-098860-6 (paperback)
    1. Proposal writing in business. 2. Business report writing. I. Title: 1 page proposal.
  II. Title.

HF5718.5 .R55 2002
651.7'8—dc21   2002023703

06 ❖/QW 10 9 8 7 6 5

FOR MAXIMILIAN AND JOANNA

Acknowledgments

I wish to thank Adnan Khashoggi for the numerous courtesies extended to me over the years and for his good advice concerning many matters, not the least of which was the importance of knowing how to write a one-page proposal.

I owe more than I can express to the thoughtful and unwavering support of my wife, Roberta Smith Riley. Ours is a proposition of loving that has lasted twenty-five years and so far has defied a description on one page, so I won't start here.

Curtis Firestone and Jean Myers have assisted in the preparation of this book in many important ways beyond the call of duty as a trusted part of our company. They proved invaluable sounding boards for some of the best ideas in the book.

Messrs. Bob Anderson and Ted Parker deserve credit for their tutorship. I know of no one else who combines good law with good scholarship in such a satisfactory manner. Finally, thanks to Bill Butler, a superb writer; Cal Morgan at ReganBooks, "the best editor"; and Judith Regan, a great publisher, who encouraged this book from the start.

CONTENTS

Chapter 1

THE BIRTH OF AN IDEA

In the mid-1980s, when I was a thirty-seven-year-old businessman, Adnan Khashoggi, one of the richest men in the world, invited me to Monte Carlo to join him aboard his yacht. We were to discuss a business proposition my company had presented to him a few months earlier. I had met Khashoggi some time before at the Mount Kenya Safari Club, where we were introduced by a mutual friend. Khashoggi is a uniquely personable and gracious man. I enjoyed his company immensely and admired his obvious success in international business. I was looking forward to doing business with him. But here in Monaco two years later, getting around to business took a while. I was his guest at the Hotel de Paris in Monaco for nearly a week as I awaited my turn in his schedule. Khashoggi was a great host to me and his numerous guests, ranging from the King of Jordan to the actress Brooke Shields. He sent me to spend my days at Cap d'Antibes, swimming and boating along the French Riviera. This was the kind of waiting I could get used to.

Finally it was time for our business meeting . . . at one o'clock in the morning. We met aboard his yacht in the Monte Carlo harbor. I was prepared for an in-depth discussion of the elaborate business plan my brother and I had sent to him a few months earlier concerning our company's activities in the Horn of Africa. I was prepared for detailed questions about the intricacies of our proposal, which concerned an equipment dealership I wanted to develop as a joint venture. Khashoggi had other ideas. "I asked for this meeting," he said, "because I wanted to teach you something very important to me, that could be very important to you—how to write a one-page business proposal."

Those few words put me on alert: obviously I had made some kind of mistake with my business plan. At first I was shocked. Like most businessmen, I was trained to be thorough, meticulous, and detailed in my presentations. I hadn't expected that my fifty-page proposal could possibly have been considered too lengthy, but obviously it was. I wondered, was this my cue to thank him for his time and leave?

Apparently not. Not only was Khashoggi not pushing me out the door, he couldn't have been more friendly, and it was apparent that he was in earnest: he really wanted me to understand what he was trying to say. I listened intently as Khashoggi continued. "The one-page proposal has been one of the keys to my business success, and it can be invaluable to you, too. Few decision-makers can ever afford to read more than one page when deciding if they are interested in a deal or not. This is even more true for people of a different culture or language."

The message was gracefully delivered and clear: the proposal I had prepared was not suited for a man like Khashoggi—not because it lacked thoroughness but because it lacked brevity! Following common practice, our original proposal was divided into sections—Company, Business, Risk Factors, Markets, Capitalization, Financial, Management, Recent Events, Legal, and References—and included dozens of diagrams, charts, and maps. But in preparing it, I quickly realized, we had failed to recognize an important fact about our target audience—Khashoggi simply couldn't take the time to digest our exhaustive proposal and make a decision. His days were measured in minutes, not hours. Even fifty pages—short by conventional business-plan standards—would take too long to read for a man who bought and sold businesses and moved capital all around the world before breakfast.

Khashoggi explained that he was motivated to help us for several reasons: he already had business dealings in the region, he liked us and our general idea, and, of course, he had the money. (According to his biographer, at that time Khashoggi had direct investments in fifteen hundred enterprises and was earning two hundred thousand dollars a day *in interest* from his uninvested capital.) He had been enthusiastic and ready to move forward—until our elaborate, overwrought proposal gave him second thoughts and frustrated his ability to make a decision. By the time I met with him, he had gotten the proposal off his desk, passing it along to lower-level advisers for evaluation.

The more subtle implication of Khashoggi's advice was that in the international arena, key decision-makers may evaluate proposals differently from their American counterparts. A complete business plan might frustrate them because their language skills are not fluent or because American-style charts, graphs, and technical detail are simply not an everyday part of their business culture. Logically such a person would refer more demanding proposals to subordinates, as Khashoggi had done—taking the proposal off the front burner, perhaps for good.

Adnan Khashoggi, having grown tired of passing on potentially good ideas, took the time to advise me on how to improve my chances. And so that night, aboard the most beautiful yacht in the world, one of the world's wealthiest men carefully laid out for me the essence of writing a business proposal that a businessperson like him could read, digest, and act on *immediately*. For him the answer was a one-page proposal that described simply and clearly the structure of the deal and what he as a venture capitalist was being asked to do. Khashoggi knew what he was talking about, for he himself had successfully made similar proposals to kings, presidents, and the CEOs of the largest multinational corporations on earth. In two hours he became a teacher and a friend. I left his company at about 3 A.M. and returned home to San Francisco with a newfound prescription for success.

The secret I learned from Khashoggi has since brought me revenues of over ten million dollars. I have used the principle he suggested to advance my business interests at home and overseas, to develop business ventures in the United States and Japan, and even to advance the private interests of my family.

Though I feel evangelical about my methods, I have kept the one-page proposal concept a secret for years, despite using it as a key element of my business style. I even improved on it after carefully studying famous one-page proposals in history—from the Magna Carta and the Declaration of Independence to the Arecibo interstellar message sent into deep space.

Then, recently, something happened that made me decide to share the secret and write this book. On behalf of one of my clients, Fuji Photo Film of Tokyo, I had a meeting with the president of one of Silicon Valley's great technology companies. I arrived and was seated in his office while he finished up a call. Glancing around his office, I noticed on his credenza a stack of more than forty proposals—solicitations from other companies, entrepreneurs, and even some from within his own company. They were slick proposals, no doubt filled with wonderful ideas, with charts and graphs illustrating all manner of brilliant points. All at once I realized what all these proposals had in common—they were unread!

Thinking back to that night in Monaco, I realized that the one-page proposal was a tool that could expedite ventures not only with the wealthiest people in the world but with businesspeople in all walks of life. I wondered how those proposal writers would feel if they knew their carefully constructed presentations were buried, unread, and likely to remain so. So many good ideas that would never take root; so much time lost; so much energy wasted; so much venture capital that would never find its way to worthy hands. I thought of my friends—businessmen, investment bankers, Hollywood producers, writers, young people with ideas for their companies—whose lengthy proposals were languishing in the backwaters of executive suites because the people for whom they were intended were too task-saturated to read them. And it was then that I knew the secret Khashoggi had shared with me should be shared with entrepreneurs everywhere, to help them convey their important propositions quickly, powerfully, and persuasively to the busy men and women who could make them happen.

The world today is experiencing an information avalanche, and it's burying any number of worthy ideas and innovators whose talents and business minds may outstrip their communication skills. Effective two-way communication can seem nearly impossible when indiscriminate mass e-mails, automated telephone solicitations, junk mail, and relentless advertising messages eclipse the possible benefits of new channels of communication. At the same time, competition for capital and other project sponsorship has increased substantially in almost every field of endeavor. Any new strategy designed to help people cut through the cacophony of data and bring some fresh air to the proposal process can only improve the flow of business everywhere.

So I wrote this book.

As you will discover, the one-page proposal has historical antecedents. Its basic formula has been used by Caesar, Napoleon, Thomas Jefferson, and Lincoln in the past and by NASA to communicate with otherworldly beings in the future. As I write these words, President Bush, through the Defense Department, has issued a request, as reported by Reuters, asking for antiterror proposals—in the very same format I recommend.

PENTAGON SEEKS A FEW GOOD IDEAS TO FIGHT TERRORISM
10/25/01

WASHINGTON—The Pentagon appealed to Americans on Thursday to send in bright ideas on thwarting terrorism, announcing an unusual, open competition to speed the winners into use.

The goal was to find concepts that can be developed and fielded in 12 to 18 months, a blink of an eye compared with standard Pentagon acquisition and deployment procedures.

Laying out a streamlined three-step application process, the Pentagon called for one-page idea descriptions by Dec. 23. Those retained will be asked to provide up to 12 pages of details.

His demands make intuitive sense. He's in hurry-up mode, so he wants everyone's best thinking, and he's not in the mood to waste time with superfluous details.

While we can't compare the tragedy of September 11 to normal business transactions, we can't escape the conclusion that in the modern business world, direct paths to action are at a similar premium. There is a need for speed out there that sometimes makes every decision seem like an emergency. It's unrealistic to think that key decision-makers will alter their normal decision-making speed when considering new ideas that cross their desks.

The one-page proposal is a time-sensitive document. Not only is it a quick read, it contains all the crucial data needed to make a decision. I didn't say that today's movers and shakers were *only* fast; they're also smart, and they absorb new material quickly so they can apply it to their battlefield view of the world.

In the pages ahead you will learn how to write a one-page proposal yourself. I think you will find it a perfect communication tool for most proposal situations in your business and private life and, apart from the outcomes of your financial ventures, that it can have fascinating, unexpected benefits for you as a person.

Like all processes, it's a journey, so let's get started.

Chapter 2

THE ONE-PAGE PROPOSAL

What Is It?

Here is my definition. The One-Page Proposal is a document that:

⇨ Succinctly expresses all the facts, reasoning, and conditions surrounding an undertaking or project

⇨ Uses persuasive language to build a case for approval

⇨ Proposes a specific course of action

⇨ Fulfills all these qualifications within a single printed page

The objective of the proposal is to convince a specific person to undertake a specific course of action. Its format is designed to encourage the reader, whose time is precious, to see the project through the eyes of the writer who originated the idea. Its parts are codified, and its language is precise in the service of brevity but not to the exclusion of understanding. Each paragraph of the One-Page Proposal serves to support and promote the desired action.

The One-Page Proposal is a template, a step-by-step procedure to accomplish your aim. It contains a distillation of ideas, plans, analysis, and action steps that, if explored completely in written form, might extend to hundreds of pages.

The One-Page Proposal is also a process. The process involves not only a comprehensive understanding of the subject at hand but also workable verbal skills, intuition, discipline, and a faith in the clarity that comes from keeping things simple. The preparation of a successful One-Page Proposal is an exercise in expressing complex thought in very few words.

Like many successful businessmen, Adnan Khashoggi relies on his instincts, knowledge, and extensive experience to guide him. For him and others of his wealth and alacrity, a two-hundred-page business plan is almost an insult; it implies that he needs overwhelming data before feeling comfortable risking investment in a business venture. Even before it is read, a printed proposal that is deliberately short says a lot to a man of Khashoggi's stature. It conveys that the preparer has respect for his time. It demonstrates that the preparer recognizes the extent of his knowledge and experience. It gives him credit for being able to absorb information and act quickly and decisively.

The law of "easiest decision" says that when confronted with a long list of decisions to be made, people tend to make the easiest decisions first. Anything that requires further study or meetings or more data gets pushed back. Too much information can delay a decision, not accelerate it.

Worldwide competition for capital or other sponsorship of major projects in engineering and construction, philanthropy, the arts, science and technology, and medicine, to name a few, has mushroomed in the last twenty years. The likelihood that support for your idea will come from your own hometown is small, and if you have a career as an entrepreneur, at some point along the way you will be obliged to seek financial, political, and/or diplomatic support from elsewhere in the world. Therefore you must take into account the language and cultural difficulties that a complex business plan might create. The One-Page Proposal has already proved to be a wonderful solution to this business problem. People and companies with superior tools of communication like the One-Page Proposal are cutting through the glut and getting their propositions funded.

Your goal is to present a task that seems as easy as possible. Therefore the final result must be exactly one page and no more. Why not one and a half, some might ask? Why not two? Sorry, it's one or nothing. Once the proposal extends past the first page, the battle is lost. Chances are, if it's more than one page, even the *first* page will not be read. All the elegance that comes from condensing the salient points of a proposal onto one page is lost when the format is violated. Why disqualify yourself before you've even had a chance?

The work involved in compressing your pitch into one page can be an important step in developing your own understanding of your project, perfecting a concise oral presentation when needed, and honing your style as a communicator. Writing a One-Page Proposal can help you identify a clear objective, focus on it, ferret out pitfalls, sharpen your thinking, and pitch an idea perfectly. Every aspect of your business life can benefit from this process.

Think of the One-Page Proposal as a photograph—one complete image composed deliberately for one frame. Given the option, would you take a picture of your family that cut out your two youngest children because they were standing outside the frame? Of course not. Likewise, to relegate the last few elements of your pitch to a second page looks like bad planning. It devalues and fragments the composition to the point where the whole idea is lost.

One page of about four hundred words in length will take an average reader three or four minutes to review. It's those few minutes of mindshare that you're after. Your reward is the accomplishment of the first, and perhaps most important, objective in the proposal game—getting your idea onto the radar screen of your target reader.

What's Wrong with the Traditional Business Plan?

There's nothing wrong with a full-scale business plan. A start-up business or any venture involving financial investment needs one—about half the time. In my own experience, most of the time I can go from my One-Page Proposal to a full agreement without ever resorting to a traditional business plan. The traditional business plan, if needed, is a specific kind of document that fulfills a specific function later in the process. A traditional business plan is not the best document to use in today's business climate to introduce an idea or a course of action to an investor, supporter, or business facilitator. For all the reasons we've discussed, it has long since outlived its utility as an *introductory* document. Nowadays it is much less likely to be read by CEOs or investors than by their teams of lawyers and accountants.

If you're already in the middle of an extensive business plan, don't let me dissuade you; go ahead and finish it—you might need it eventually. But remember that once you're done, the only smart thing to do is to go back and do it again—in one page.

What the One-Page Proposal *Isn't*

The One-Page Proposal is similar to other short-form business documents. It is something like an executive summary; a little like the "blue book" busy politicians use to brief themselves about the concerns of a particular constituency; even a little like the cover page of an investment prospectus.

But here's the difference: while those document forms are short, only the One-Page Proposal is an actual *proposal*. The others are simply abridgments. They do not engage, persuade, or ask for anything. The executive summary, for example, is just a short report presenting the status quo. Its language is declarative, not persuasive. A blue book is an edited-for-time document that reaches brevity by excluding rather than compressing. It communicates only what is absolutely necessary for a certain audience in a certain window of time. And the cover sheet of a prospectus summarizes the key points of an investment but proposes nothing.

The One-Page Proposal delivers all the necessary information its reader needs to make a decision, as well as the all-important pitch. It is not a cut-down version of a longer document; *it is a complete entity in and of itself.* Remember, you are being given a template—a formula that is repeatable. If you do not follow the formula and use all its parts, you don't have a proposal—you just have a short report.

The One-Page Proposal is an instrument of initiation. It gets things started. Inertia is the most powerful force in business. Things stay just as they are until something—brute force, reason, fear, enlightened self-interest, the survival instinct—effects movement. The One-Page Proposal sets things in motion by proposing something new in a way that seems doable and defies the reader's instinct toward remaining in a static environment.

So what do you want to do? Start a youth soccer league? The One-Page Proposal is the perfect document to present to your city council, to your parks department, or to youth ministries in your neighborhood. In one page you can lay out your plans, the key reasons why the soccer league is important, necessary financial and community resources, the time frame enabling a warm-weather start, and what each person and organization in the community can do to make it happen.

Let's think bigger. Do you want to start a new business? Do you need investors to make it happen? Send the One-Page Proposal to each carefully selected potential investor to start your search for capital.

Let's think really big: you want to lure a National Football League team to your city. It's going to take a coordinated marshaling of political figures, businesspeople, banking interests, state legislators, bonding authorities, and heavyweight community leaders to pull this off. Eventually a whopping business plan will be needed for all parties to read and understand. But first your vision, knowledge, and passion for this project must be communicated to those key players in town who can set the greater community wheels rolling. These are important people you need to convince, and they don't have time for outlandish ideas. Your One-Page Proposal shows the logic, the viability, the financial underpinnings, and the heady possibilities of your idea—and does so efficiently.

Not every idea is that grand in scale. Thankfully, the One-Page Proposal format lends itself to the complete range of business and "civilian" activities—a new job, a new community project, an expedition, a request for philanthropy, a grant request, a request for sales consideration, a bid for historic preservation, or an idea for public transportation improvement. I once used a One-Page Proposal to create a job for myself in a great company—and my résumé wasn't even needed until later, almost as a formality. *Anything* can be proposed effectively using the One-Page Proposal format.

There are certain industries out there whose proposal document forms are so entrenched and whose rules are so prescribed that the One-Page Proposal may not be appropriate or will be rejected on form alone. There aren't many, and you simply have to be aware when a company's proposal policies are inviolable. I've only run into three or four areas in which the One-Page Proposal has been rejected on form:

⇨ *Government proposals*
Proposals submitted to state or federal government (George Bush's recent request notwithstanding) have a certain form, length, and sequence of information that is proprietary and unique to each branch of government. It is fruitless to try to force a One-Page Proposal into that machinery.

⇨ *Some grant proposals*
Foundations and other granting authorities often provide their own forms to those who wish to apply for funds or propose new ideas.

⇨ *Major community development proposals*
Proposals that involve public/private funding, architecture, engineering/ construction, environmental impact studies, statute review, EEOC compliance, and so on, are so complex in nature that even a severe abridgment of the deal elements is just not possible in one page. But let me add that even here a One-Page Proposal might be a perfectly appropriate document with which to initiate the idea for a project that assumes massive scale later.

⇨ *Literary proposals*
These are traditionally lengthy, and there are other guides with advice on how to craft an effective book idea. However, it is not impossible to imagine a One-Page Proposal that lands on an editor's desk and is intriguing enough to elicit a request for a traditional proposal from the author. See the One-Page Proposal for this book on page 100.

I don't believe there are many companies today that unequivocally ban proposals that don't fit their preconceived ideas of what a proposal should look like. The field is wide open—use the One-Page Proposal everywhere except in those situations where you are *certain* a unique form is required.

What About Expensive Production Values?

One of the promises of the Internet is that small businesses—even tiny ones—can compete with the big boys. That promise drove the website creation business in the 1990s. If your website makes you look big, well, then, in a very real sense, you are big.

The One-Page Proposal can have a similar effect.

Executed properly, the One-Page Proposal can be an enormously effective means of business communication. Its power does not derive from being handsomely bound, from being printed in full color on expensive paper, or from being adorned with the cutting-edge graphic design with which big companies suggest their size, wealth, and stature. Its power derives from knowledge imparted succinctly. Any person or company, regardless of size, wealth, or location, can produce a One-Page Proposal and accomplish a necessary part of competitive business practice—getting into the game.

The One-Page Proposal is a great counterbalance to the standard and erroneous preconception regarding business materials in general: that the more expensive the packaging, the better. Pricey packaging only goes so far, and in today's climate that's often nowhere. Flashy production values cost a fortune in designers and printing, and for what? To create a great first impression? To make a company seem bigger than it is? The One-Page Proposal changes that game by substituting substance for flash. An engaging format replaces fancier packaging, and laserlike clarity replaces predictable business bromides.

So It's Quick to Read; Is It Quick to Write?

What kind of situation are you in? Are you pressed for time, eager for a shortcut, hoping the short format of the One-Page Proposal might save you some work? If so, the One-Page Proposal process may not be right for you. It may seem as though a single page can be written easily or in a hurry, but the fact is that the One-Page Proposal can take some time. It's not nearly as long to prepare as a full business plan, but it's not a one-hour job, either. To do a responsible job condensing all your information into a one-page format, you've first got to amass, evaluate, prioritize, and master every bit of information.

If you're in a time bind, I can't think of any proposal format that will *save* you, but the internal dynamics of the One-Page Proposal *can* be completed quickly if your proposal involves information with which you are already familiar. Perhaps the subject of your proposal concerns an area in which you are considered an expert. If you come to the table with comprehensive knowledge and the critical factors for a convincing proposal—such as background facts, rationale, finances, and course of action—then the One-Page Proposal is a natural vehicle with which to forward your interests quickly. The majority of your time can be spent on the wording of the proposal, tailoring it in just the right way to your reader, rather than on original research. The proposal can be on your target reader's desk in a matter of days, not weeks. So if you're an expert, the One-Page Proposal is your very best choice for making a fast, effective, substantial proposal when time is short.

This is very important: The One-Page Proposal won't save a bad or sloppy idea. It is not designed to sell defective products to unwitting buyers. It won't make something worthless appear to be valuable. It won't make last year's idea into the Next Big Thing. It won't make something bad sound good just because you said it quickly and well. But it can help you discern when there's something wrong with your pitch. The One-Page Proposal works when your idea makes sense and when the course of action you propose is the right course for everyone. It's a tool, and like all good tools it works beautifully when applied to the proper situation. Even the best screwdriver in the world won't drive nails.

We have explored the One-Page Proposal's benefits for the reader/recipient, but it has value for the writer, too, whether the proposal is accepted or declined. I believe the preparation and writing of the One-Page Proposal is the most valuable process anyone, in any transaction, can undertake. As you will see when we get into the specifics of execution, the One-Page Proposal requires preparation and research; it requires understanding your subject so thoroughly that no speculation or ambiguity remains. It imposes a program of self-evaluation that leads to a mastery of the subject, powerful persuasive language in the proposal, and confidence in a positive outcome.

The One-Page Proposal process will encourage you to be articulate but concise; broadly informed but sharply selective in what you present; confident in your proposal's strengths but aware of its weaknesses; passionate and aggressive but mindful of the importance of proportion and grace.

Moreover, the practice of crafting such efficient documents can only foster your own diligence and ability to concentrate on seeing a task through to completion. A good One-Page Proposal cannot be dashed off while driving your car. Neither can it be spoken haphazardly into a Dictaphone. Through thinking, then researching, then writing, then refining, even already skilled communicators will find their evaluative and expressive abilities heightened immensely.

Chapter 3

PREPARATION

Be Cool, Calm, and Collected

Preparation is the key to success with the One-Page Proposal. Preparation implies time—time to research all the facts and figures you will need, and time to learn all you need to know about the recipient of your proposal. Yes, time is a luxury, and ironically, I've developed the One-Page Proposal in large part because time is an ever-shrinking commodity. Logically, however, by putting in time at the beginning to structure your argument strategically, write it articulately, and review it objectively, you decrease the time your reader will have to contribute to understanding it later on.

Your mental outlook is important from the beginning; you need to feel confident about the quality of your work. Trying to get by on insufficient data will make you feel the way you did in college when you faked your way through reports on books you hadn't read. It's not a good feeling, and it will manifest itself in ill-conceived objectives, unanticipated pitfalls, or sloppy writing. Calm, not panic, leads to thorough completion of a project. Don't allow loose ends or holes in your research; put in the extra time as part of your preparation. Don't set unrealistic deadlines for yourself. In fact, don't set a deadline at all. Your One-Page Proposal should not be sent out into the world until it is perfect, no matter what the day is on your calendar.

How you start preparing to write your One-Page Proposal depends entirely on what you know already. You have to establish exactly what information is lacking and then fill those gaps through research. For example, many proposals originate with people who have ideas for improving a preexisting process, product, work practice, or manufacturing method. Ideas for improvement nearly always come from people who know a great deal about the situation they're trying to improve, usually from firsthand experience. If that's your situation, you may be able to write the majority of your One-Page Proposal based on your own knowledge. Your research, therefore, may be confined to certain financial details—a fact or figure here or there. The One-Page Proposal calls for very specific facts and figures, so this book will clarify which financial details you need to attend to.

Perhaps your knowledge is complete, but you don't know the best person to present your proposal to. Your work then becomes a research project to find that target person. Again, we'll discuss the method for finding a reader in the pages ahead. The important point to absorb here is that the recipient of the One-Page Proposal determines to a great extent what you say and how you say it. The best proposals start with a specific recipient in mind, and play to that person's style and interests.

The most diligent preparation will fall to those who have an important idea to pitch but do not possess the concrete facts and figures upon which to build a persuasive argument. In your gut you may know your idea is timely, appropriate, and beneficial, but you lack the "chapter and verse" to convince others who may not share your insight. You have the largest job ahead, and the following information is mostly for you.

Do Some Accumulating

Here is a good first step: While keeping in mind your objective, take an inventory of the things around you that could be source material for your One-Page Proposal. This is probably a topic that will have interested you for some time. Either you have already gathered all the pertinent business documentation about it into a file, or you know where to find it. Go ahead and assemble the documents that will form the research basis of your proposal. What will this include? Among other things, newspaper articles, magazine articles, Internet documents, government studies, industry data and publications, photographs, charts and statistics, census data, demographic data, Gallup polls, photocopies, books, and your own notes.

Continue your preparation by making two lists. First, list all the things you know about what you plan to propose—not what you suspect or what you've heard, but what you *know*. That means firsthand, or at least confirmed, information about the industry you're concerned with, the company you're targeting, the person you're targeting within it, and the prices and costs that your project is likely to entail. You must be honest with yourself about the confidence level or certainty with which you hold this knowledge. It is essential that this list be complete, because it leads to the more important list—the list of things you *don't* know. Understanding the width and breadth of your lack of knowledge is the true starting point for your research.

A good friend of mine and his brother run a large family construction business in North Carolina. About five years ago their company, working with a famous professor from Chicago, perfected the design of a solar roof that could have wide application for energy generators and builders all over the world. The family knew a lot about construction, having built homes, factories, and schools all along the Atlantic seaboard. They had firsthand knowledge of the electric power–generating industry and knew how their company's technology could be used to heat homes in the winter and provide power for air conditioners in the summer. They knew that the economics of this solar roof would represent tremendous savings to homeowners all over the world. On the other hand, they did not know much about the solar energy segment of power generation. They put this on their "don't know" list, along with the:

⇨ Size and shape of the market

⇨ Regulatory agencies responsible for solar energy

⇨ Particular multinational companies that have strategies to exploit the solar market

They were invited to pitch their invention to Duke Energy, a major publicly traded power company in their home state of North Carolina. They knew quite a bit about Duke by reputation, but in order to supplement their knowledge, they called Duke's investor relations department and had the most recent annual report sent to them. Spurred on by their success as detectives, the brothers found creative answers to all their "don't knows," even though the product itself was an undeniable winner, and the pressure was high to market their breakthrough before someone else did.

Don't worry if your "don't know" list is long at the beginning. My suggestion is that you make both lists as long as possible. Give yourself credit for knowing even small things that may prove very important down the road. At the same time, understand that the proposal will come together more easily and naturally now that you know where the gaps are. In fact, a lot of the missing information is probably to be found in a careful rereading of the materials you already have in your possession.

T. S. Eliot said, "All our knowledge brings us nearer to our ignorance," a very healthy attitude to bring to the process. Be honest. Do the work. There's a lot to learn, and a lot to impart to your target reader.

Your Goal Is Complete Understanding

The goal of your research is mastery of the subject—the kind of comprehension that allows you to express yourself clearly, simply, and with great impact and confidence. Much of your research will involve the aggregation of dry facts and figures, but the tone and style of your written representations will reflect your understanding of the project and your comfort with the material. This means that everything you learn during the course of your research is beneficial, even if it extends beyond the strict number of topics on your "don't know" list.

This is not a test; don't focus solely on your list. Take in all the information you can. You may find a tangential but suddenly important tidbit bubbling to the surface in unexpected ways later, when you are actually writing the One-Page Proposal. Your passion for your topic will provide the energy for this research. If you really care deeply about the proposal you're making, taking the time to construct a powerful argument is a pleasure, not forced labor.

The World Wide Web is like a library containing all the books in the world—all in a big heap on the floor. In other words, the Web is so full of information that it defies organization. Much industry-specific data, statistics, projections, news, and information pertinent to your One-Page Proposal can be found on the Internet—the trick is knowing how to find it in an efficient, timely manner. If you don't have Internet access at your home or office, the closest public library can have you on-line on its machines in minutes.

Here are a few tips to help you locate what you need:

⇨ Start big. Broadly search your topic by using any of the popular Internet search engines. Both Google (www.google.com) and Yahoo! (www.yahoo.com) have worked well for me.

⇨ Try to follow the normal Boolean protocols (e.g. "and," "or," "and not") to home in on a particular subject. If you are unfamiliar with this search language, it's quite easy to get it from your Internet provider.

⇨ Look for industry and commercial data using federal government websites. I've had great luck with this—there is an unbelievable abundance of information available within the public domain. Try these comprehensive government sites as starting points for broad research, information, and data/statistics.

➡ www.business.gov

The Small Business Administration created this site as a repository of federal government information for small businesses. Main topics include doing business with the government; financial/loan advice; general business guidelines for start-ups; international trade; labor and employment issues; and federal laws and regulations.

➡ www.fedworld.gov

This large and comprehensive repository of federal government information provides links to government agencies, government branches, departments, courts, commissions, embassies, and other government sites ad infinitum.

➡ www.fedworld.gov/detail.htm#search

The FedWorld search engine can locate data and further links from the whole FedWorld system.

➡ www.worldtec.fedworld.gov/index.htm

This site translates into English news about business, science, and technology around the world. Available by subscription.

➡ www.fedstats.gov

The FedStats site provides a remarkable search engine that finds and retrieves statistics published by U.S. government agencies. This site also offers summarized information from the *Statistical Abstract*.

➡ www.info.gov

The purpose of this large, complex site, ironically, is to simplify access to government information. The site has five pillars: the InQuery search engine to government and military databases, a federal directory, a directory of popular consumer categories, international links, and the Federal Information Center.

➡ www.access.gpo.gov

This is the U.S. Government Printing Office home page ("Keeping America Informed"). The GPO provides access to government documents such as Supreme Court decisions and congressional records and bills.

If you prefer pre–World Wide Web forms of research, there are still dozens of ways to find what you need. Do it the easy way first: meet with a reference librarian and ask for exactly the information you desire. Library professionals today are well armed with research tools, and they're generally great sleuths. They will most likely present you with some large, intimidating books, but take heart—they're far more negotiable than they appear. Here's a crash course:

`SIC codebooks`—The Standard Industry Classification system categorizes every industry in the United States by a number code that reveals its market, its size, and other specifics. This is a great way to establish a conceptual framework for your idea and to learn about competitors, potential partners, distributors, the financial dimensions of the industry, and the associations that govern or promote the industry. A leading publisher of SIC books is the *Thomas Register*.

`Annual reports`—Libraries often contain current copies of public and private companies' annual reports. This is where you find not only facts and figures but also the language that's used to describe hard numbers in a specific industry. In addition, annual reports provide a sense of the competition and market strategies. If your library is limited, you can find virtually any annual report on-line. Try these websites:

⇨ www.annualreportslibrary.com

⇨ www.thecorporatelibrary.com

⇨ www.reportgallery.com

⇨ www.cfonews.com

⇨ www.10-kwizard.com. This site is especially useful for finding the valuable information on people, companies, and industries that lurks deep in Securities and Exchange Commission filings. Forms include virtually all public companies' 10K and 10Q forms, registration statements, proxies, information statements, and quarterly and annual reports. This is a subscription service, but it can be worth it.

Association journals and magazines—Every large national industry is supported by an association that lobbies in Washington and publishes newsletters and magazines of topical interest to its members. These are a great source of industry data, trends, and even information on specific executives.

Government regulatory agency bulletins—These offer a variety of industry data, including industry trends and problems plaguing an industry.

All the above are available to the public at little or no cost. Private business information services can provide additional data at considerable cost. These services include financial reporting firms like Dun & Bradstreet and Moody's and broad information services like Nexus.

Who Gets the One-Page Proposal?

Do you have a specific person in mind to receive your One-Page Proposal? That's important information to have right from the beginning because it helps shape the content and tone of your writing. If you know the individual personally, then your knowledge of your reader's interests, habits, and demeanor can be a major advantage in communicating persuasively.

If you know the intended recipient's name but not much else, do some research:

⇨ Do a name search in the archive of the newspaper in your target reader's home city. There may be articles with business and biographical information.

⇨ Talk to industry or social peers who know your target personally or professionally.

⇨ Check *Who's Who* for an entry on this person. If he or she is a company executive, you may find additional material in annual reports or company brochures.

⇨ Check with the company's PR department and see if there are any recent press releases with his or her name referenced. Sometimes PR can supply a press release with great biographical and background information, including recent promotions.

Once you know a little about the person, use what you have learned to create a strategic attitude in your proposal that fits the reader's personality and interests. Use your research to anticipate the reactions of your targeted reader. For example, if you are pitching a movie idea to a longtime film financier, be specific and brief about how film profits will be generated—he already knows all about that. On the other hand, if you are approaching foreign investors who are unfamiliar with the nature of the business, a little more explanation might go a long way toward bolstering their confidence both in the investment and in you.

What if you know the company or organization that deserves your proposal but not the right person in it?

⇨ Call the company and ask. Try the PR department first, then receptionists or secretaries.

⇨ Read trade publications and see who within the company is quoted as an authority in your area of interest.

⇨ Call anyone who has worked with the company, specifically the company's ad agency or law firm, especially if you have a connection there.

Keep in mind that your One-Page Proposal may be appropriate for dozens of people. Don't limit yourself to someone you know or the same few powerful, wealthy people in your town who are constantly approached for investment. Robert Noyce, the founder of Intel, once said, "Don't be encumbered by history; just do something wonderful." Aim high. A wide circle of friends helps, but think beyond your current horizons. Great men and women are always interested in new, well-thought-out ideas that will make them more successful. There's an old saying: Good business makes fast friends. Approach everyone—your excitement will be contagious.

Keeping It Personal

When I was a young man of twenty-two traveling through Turkey, I picked up a copy of *Newsweek* and read an article describing the extraordinary life and conservation efforts of two Americans: actor William Holden and his best friend, Don Hunt. The picture alongside the article showed the two men running through the tall grass of Kenya chasing a cheetah. The article described their life at the Mount Kenya Safari Club and their vision for the club's expansion. It was 1969, and most of my friends were serving in the armed forces; several were in Vietnam, and two of them had been killed in action. I felt lucky to be declared 4F as a result of a serious football injury, but I felt a certain sense of responsibility to use this reprieve as an opportunity to do something valuable with my life. The *Newsweek* article was my call to action.

I traveled to Kenya and spent the next four months studying every detail of Holden's and Hunt's lives—their businesses and their private concerns. Finally I called Don Hunt to make an appointment to see him, and to make him an offer he couldn't refuse—to hire me! I called Nanyuki, where the Mount Kenya Safari Club is located, using a two-way radio and the word "over" after each complete thought. The conversation was awkward, to say the least, but because I knew the action I wanted (a meeting) and because I had thought out my proposition to the last detail, I got that meeting. Within five months I was on safari in the Horn of Africa with Holden and Hunt, catching wild animals in a relocation effort in Somalia. I was a long way from home and it was my first job, but I loved it. I worked for them for six years, sometimes catching cheetah in Somalia, other times building drive-through safari parks for the likes of Warner Brothers. It was a great time in my life during which I enjoyed wonderful adventures, and I owe it all to the effort I put into my initial proposition.

The point is this: Carefully select the person you plan to take your proposal to, and always remember that business is personal. I had a hunch that Holden and Hunt would respect my effort to meet them—and I was right.

I found out later that thousands of people had written Holden and Hunt asking for jobs and sending résumés, but I was the only one who had traveled to Kenya to meet them. That trip was the extra mile, and it changed my life.

It is virtually a given that the person you have identified as the ideal recipient of your proposal has a track record in business, philanthropy, investments, or decision-making. Learn about those dealings and how the person played a role in them. This is strategic research—the kind of information that can really make a difference in your proposal.

You may know, for example, that the venture capitalist to whom you are presenting your One-Page Proposal has negotiated several deals similar to yours in the past. In researching those past deals, you might discover that this major player never—*ever*—invests in start-ups that do not have a qualified chief financial officer on board. This is golden information. Before presenting your proposal, you can make sure you have a solid financial officer on your side, and use their name prominently in the proposal.

Find out if your investor has an altruistic bent. Be willing to accommodate his or her taste by adding a philanthropic or charitable component to your proposal. You've given it a better chance for approval, and you've benefited society as well as your own pocket. If you know that your target reader has not been receptive to proposals similar to yours in the past, demonstrate how the landscape has changed since those proposals, and show how your new proposal solves all the problems to which your recipient once objected.

For example, let's say you're proposing a new summer concert series for your city's biggest public park. The mayor has to authorize your plan, and she's likely to say no because a previous concert series held there was a financial disaster—no one showed up. Instead of ignoring this knowledge, meet her probable objections head-on: "The problems that caused the financial failure of previous SummerFests have been overcome. Park crime has been virtually eliminated; park attendance is up 300 percent; the surrounding neighborhood has improved demographically; a professional promotions firm has agreed to handle advertising pro bono; and major rock bands have already agreed to play at the site." The mayor will have a hard time saying no to that. Had you not known of her prior experience, your proposal might have gotten a quick heave-ho.

Clearly there is a strategic advantage to knowing the patterns and habits of the intended recipient of your One-Page Proposal, but don't take it to a ridiculous extreme. A recent proposal to relocate the Charlotte, North Carolina, professional basketball team to Louisville, Kentucky, for example, went a bit overboard by suggesting that, in return for millions of dollars in naming rights sold to Kentucky Fried Chicken, the new arena could be built to resemble a huge bucket of chicken, red and white graphics included. Even for KFC, which may indeed play a role in landing the team, this architectural incentive was over the top. Furthermore it was unnecessary, because it would not be in KFC's interest to offend the community.

My working assumption is always that my proposal's recipient has a sharply honed BS detector. Any incentive that seems too ingratiating, too convenient, too obviously intended to curry favor will make the whole proposal seem bogus. Your proposal will always advance based on its merits, not on an implied payback.

Factor In the Opposing Team

Never underestimate the factors working against the success of your proposal: competitive people, competitive interests, and, in the case of political projects, opposing ideologies.

Seven years ago I sent a One-Page Proposal to New York Senator Daniel Patrick Moynihan on behalf of a Japanese client—Nippon Television Network (for the complete One-Page Proposal, see page 95). They sought his endorsement of a proposal to display the space shuttle *Enterprise* at a special exhibition in Tokyo. It was a sensitive project at a sensitive time in American-Japanese relations. In doing my research on this proposal I had learned that detractors on Capitol Hill wanted to portray the proposal and its proposers as usurious, hoping only to make exorbitant profits. It was vital therefore that I convey to Senator Moynihan all the elements of the proposition, particularly the critical financial circumstances. I addressed these concerns explicitly in the One-Page Proposal. To begin the financial section I wrote, "There will be no costs to the United States. The Sponsor and other cooperating Japanese companies and Japanese government agencies will pay all costs associated with the exhibition, including costs incurred by NASM, the Smithsonian Institution, NASA, and the U.S. Navy for staff time as billed. The exhibition is an entirely nonprofit undertaking; all net proceeds will be donated to NASM and the Smithsonian." I had easily blunted the possibility of any political criticism by knowing ahead of time what that criticism would be. The project got Senator Moynihan's endorsement.

Even if your proposal is entirely benign and has no direct competitors, there will always be those who weigh against it simply because the investor's interest in your project may divert time and money away from *their* project. There is not much you can do about this except keep your ears open for disparaging or false claims made against you. If that happens, you may have to rebut in a timely manner.

Fact-Checking

As I have said, be very careful and very certain about the quality of data you derive from your research. The Internet, for example, can be a minefield of fragmentary, partial, or false information. My suggestion would be to follow the old journalistic rule and have at least two independent sources to verify the facts and figures you will use in the One-Page Proposal.

What harm can result from bad information? First, your reader may just happen to know as much as you—or even more—about the topic of your proposal. As he reads the data sections, any mistakes or errors of interpretation will surely catch his attention. This can be the kiss of death for any proposal—an immediate deal-breaker.

Second, incomplete data can lead to a false conclusion. You may assume something to be a fact based on your readings, and this fact may form the entire underlying rationale of your One-Page Proposal. Make sure the basic facts are correct before you build from them. One-Page Proposal data should be irrefutable.

Anticipate the Questions

Why are most proposals—in business and in life—turned down? Because the easiest, safest response to a proposal is *no*. *No* means no future complications, no downside, no risk. Smart, savvy investors and decision-makers say yes only when their decisions are virtually guaranteed to bring success. They don't need to take wild risks. When a winner comes their way, they'll know to take advantage of the opportunity.

The ultimate purpose of One-Page Proposal research is to anticipate every point at which the recipient might become uncomfortable, and to deflect his no with solid facts and impeccable reasoning. The best way to do this is to avoid generalizations. For example, to demonstrate to your councilmember that there is popular support for a new playground in your neighborhood, you could write, "Nearly all residents in this area support the playground plan . . . ," to which the councilmember might respond, "How do you know?" Better to write, "Based on a neighborhood canvass conducted from 6-1-01 through 7-1-01 by Jones & Associates polling firm, 89 percent of all households support . . ." The councilmember will give credit for credible facts.

Research, and hence knowledge, is the antithesis of fear. Big cost figures always get your recipient's attention and raise the fear factor. If he sees large capital expenditures, the first question to cross his mind will be, "How can that kind of money be raised, repaid, or generated?" Predict those fears, and be prepared by researching solutions. Consider creative alternatives to financial snares: "Construction costs have been quoted at $500,000. Because these funds are not in the city's current budget, the neighborhood's 5,000 residents have voted to assess themselves a $100 one-time fee to underwrite construction, leaving the city only the expense of issuing permits and improving the infrastructure at the site."

Proposal readers are trained to be poised and ready with certain queries. Here are examples of questions that cannot go unanswered:

⇨ How is the project structured?

⇨ Who will take responsibility for implementing the project?

⇨ How much will it cost?

⇨ How much will/can it earn back?

⇨ What makes your proposal unique and timely?

⇨ What specific experience do you have to offer?

Businesspeople, managers, and political leaders are not known for being impetuous. Investors will move quickly when all the deal's particulars are on the table and they feel safe and comfortable. Until then, caution is the byword. You should be so diligent in your research that your solid facts trump their natural skepticism. Never, ever give them a chance to say no.

Chapter 4

THE ROAD MAP—STARTING TO THINK IT THROUGH

Pulling It All Together

The ideal One-Page Proposal has a distinct format—eight sections, each with a specific purpose. Ultimately each will have a specific place and a general length on our one sheet of paper. For now, though, we won't worry about getting our thoughts down to one page but will concern ourselves only with recognizing these eight sections: Title, Subtitle, Target, Secondary Targets, Rationale, Financial, Status, and Action.

This sequence follows a logical and organic progression of thought and argument:

⇨ Title and Subtitle label and define the entire proposal.

⇨ Target and Secondary Targets sections identify the goals of the proposal.

⇨ Rationale lays out the basic reasons why the proposed action is necessary.

⇨ Financial puts dollars and cents to the deal.

⇨ Status states how things stand at the moment.

⇨ Action clarifies exactly what the proposer wants the recipient to do.

These are the eight ingredients of the One-Page Proposal. Like a culinary masterpiece, greatness comes from the dynamic interplay of all its parts. For best effect they must be added in sequence, in the proper proportions, each complementing the others and none left out.

A Sample One-Page Proposal

On the following page, you will find a sample One-Page Proposal. This is the proposal I use to solicit investors for my primary business, Geniisis Agents. As you can see, the major parts of the One-Page Proposal are organized north to south on a very full page (as the One-Page Proposal tends to be). The length of each part may vary in accordance with many factors—relative importance within a project, expertise of the target reader, the project's current status—but the sequence from top to bottom should always stay the same.

You will find that I have censored the exact numbers in the Status section, as this proposal is a direct replica of the one I use in real life.

GENIISIS AGENTS

Linking Intellectual Free Agents + the Hottest Companies of the 21st Century

<u>TARGET:</u> TO BE THE WORLD'S LEADING AGENCY FOR INTELLECTUAL TALENT FROM UNIVERSITIES AND RESEARCH INSTITUTIONS AROUND THE WORLD AND TO MARKET THEIR BREAKTHROUGH DISCOVERIES TO INTERESTED INDUSTRIAL PARTNERS.

- To utilize the highly valuable discoveries of intellects working in the best universities in the world by ensuring they are paired with ideal business partners.

- To develop and retain some of the most important new equities of the twenty-first century.

Knowledge is now the primary driver of productivity and economic growth in the United States and other industrialized countries. Research is pivotal to knowledge-based economies. Of the $31 billion spent on research in the United States in 1997, $21 billion, or 67 percent, was spent by universities and nonprofit research institutions. This ratio is increasing. At the heart of primary research within universities are individuals and teams of individuals who are changing the world. In 1999 Pat Riley, a San Francisco businessman with an academic background at Oxford and the University of California, formed Geniisis Agents to represent such individuals and to develop markets for their discoveries.

Geniisis Agents LLC, a privately held company in San Francisco, is emerging as the foremost representative of leading thinkers from universities and research institutes throughout the world. The Company creates a global market for its clients' discoveries by aligning extraordinary minds with extraordinary companies in eighty subject categories, including biotechnology, pharmaceuticals, advanced materials, computer software, telecommunications, and the Internet. A fully integrated corporate portal, specific to Geniisis and known as EWOKS (Enterprise-Wide Open-Ended Knowledge System), monitors and teams up talent in the best interests of both the academic and corporate clients. Geniisis operates as an agency for genius and as an agency for corporations needing to access that genius to develop new, profitable revenue streams.

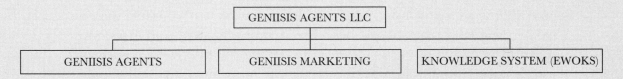

<u>FINANCIAL:</u> Geniisis Agents is a start-up being financed for growth. Revenues in all segments are expected from new equities and cash fees derived from a percentage participation in: person-to-business dealings (i.e., primary employment agreements, patent and copyright participations, and equity interests) and business-to-business dealings whereby the intellectual property has been bundled into a formal business structure or security that can be offered for sale and purchased (i.e., interests in research and development contracts, joint ventures, newly formed companies, intellectual property or intellectual property companies being spun off by others, and new companies on the verge of a public offering).

<u>STATUS:</u> The Company is in the formative stage, putting its management team together and expanding its network of fellows around the world. The Company is now seeking a financial partner to underwrite the development of Geniisis Agents. Such investment is estimated to be $▮▮▮▮▮ over three years. To date, the founder has invested $▮▮▮▮▮: $▮▮▮▮▮ in equity and $▮▮▮▮ in loans to cover organizational expenses. In addition, the investment banking firm of Petkevich & Partners has made an equity investment of $▮▮▮▮.

<u>ACTION:</u> For *potential investor X* to determine if they are interested in receiving a full and confidential presentation pursuant to a possible investment in Geniisis Agents.

Patrick G. Riley, 15 April 2002

Title

> **GENIISIS AGENTS**
> *Linking Intellectual Free Agents + the Hottest Companies of the 21st Century*

We always lead, as you would expect, with the title, in capital letters at the top of the page. Visually it signifies commencement, and it does something more: just as the One-Page Proposal condenses a much larger business plan into one page with no loss of impact, clarity, or intention, the title condenses the proposal into a single phrase. If nothing else, your reader will read this, and that's why it has to frame and accurately reflect the contents of the document.

Subtitle

> **GENIISIS AGENTS**
> *Linking Intellectual Free Agents + the Hottest Companies of the 21st Century*

The subtitle appears in upper- and lowercase letters just below the title. It is a follow-up statement that amplifies the title, giving it color and interest and adding a second layer of information and explanation. While the title is a simple label, the subtitle has to be both explanatory and expressive. Even if he or she has reservations after seeing the title, your reader will surely proceed to the subtitle, where you can hook him into reading on.

Target

> <u>*TARGET*</u>: TO BE THE WORLD'S LEADING AGENCY FOR INTELLECTUAL TALENT FROM UNIVERSITIES AND RESEARCH INSTITUTIONS AROUND THE WORLD AND TO MARKET THEIR BREAKTHROUGH DISCOVERIES TO INTERESTED INDUSTRIAL PARTNERS.

The target, consisting entirely of a target statement, could just as easily be called the *intention* because it declares, in plain language, just what the proposal intends to accomplish. In other words, in the target you are answering the reader's question "What are you trying to do?" More specifically, "What will be accomplished if this proposal goes forward?" Here you state the main goal of your proposal.

Secondary Targets

- To utilize the highly valuable discoveries of intellects working in the best universities in the world by ensuring they are paired with ideal business partners.

- To develop and retain some of the most important new equities of the twenty-first century.

Whatever project your One-Page Proposal intends to set in motion, it almost certainly has more than one objective. Secondary targets are important, but none of them alone could carry the proposal. They complement the main objective and build the case for its approval by adding to its perceived benefits. This listing of objectives or benefits has a cumulative effect; assuming the reader looks kindly upon the primary objective, the project moves from good to great as the secondary targets stress its broader payoffs.

Rationale

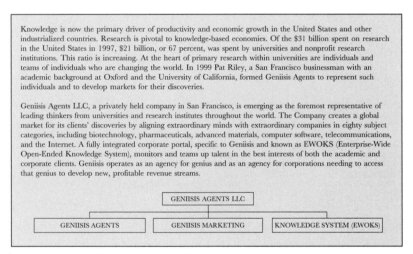

Knowledge is now the primary driver of productivity and economic growth in the United States and other industrialized countries. Research is pivotal to knowledge-based economies. Of the $31 billion spent on research in the United States in 1997, $21 billion, or 67 percent, was spent by universities and nonprofit research institutions. This ratio is increasing. At the heart of primary research within universities are individuals and teams of individuals who are changing the world. In 1999 Pat Riley, a San Francisco businessman with an academic background at Oxford and the University of California, formed Geniisis Agents to represent such individuals and to develop markets for their discoveries.

Geniisis Agents LLC, a privately held company in San Francisco, is emerging as the foremost representative of leading thinkers from universities and research institutes throughout the world. The Company creates a global market for its clients' discoveries by aligning extraordinary minds with extraordinary companies in eighty subject categories, including biotechnology, pharmaceuticals, advanced materials, computer software, telecommunications, and the Internet. A fully integrated corporate portal, specific to Geniisis and known as EWOKS (Enterprise-Wide Open-Ended Knowledge System), monitors and teams up talent in the best interests of both the academic and corporate clients. Geniisis operates as an agency for genius and as an agency for corporations needing to access that genius to develop new, profitable revenue streams.

This is "the pitch," where you *sell* your proposal, or better yet, where the proposal sells itself. In one, two, or three short paragraphs, the rationale establishes all the reasons why the project can, will, and should go forward. In this, the largest prose section of the One-Page Proposal, much of the specific research you have done comes into play. The rationale defends and supports the objectives by predicting and answering any question that the objectives may have raised in the reader's mind. Here's your chance to sound prepared and passionate.

Financial

The financial section concerns hard numbers; costs and revenues, yes, but also other kinds of financial resources that will be required to make your proposal a reality. This is the only place in the One-Page Proposal where money matters are discussed in detail. In some way, at some point, nearly every project involves financial backing—a sponsor, a third party, a bank, an investor, or a family friend. This section is where you quantify and qualify the financial commitments of the deal. It establishes the financial framework for your proposal. The reader needs to understand the financial implications of the proposal even though the reader may not necessarily be an investor. You may be asking the reader for nonfinancial support, but he will still need to understand the money issues if he is to back your proposal or take it to the people who can.

Status

Here is your opportunity to answer the following questions: What is the situation now? What has been done to date? What elements of the deal are already in place? Who has been talked to? Have any agreements already been signed? Outline exactly where the deal stands on the very day the proposal is set before the reader. Being up-to-date is invaluable—be prepared to change this paragraph every day as the project progresses.

Action

Your action statement is basically the answer to your reader's implied question "What can I do for you?" Everything you have written in the One-

Page Proposal so far has been in preparation for this crucial sentence. Obviously you must be specific about what you want—whether it's a recommendation, an investment, a loan, or a personal commitment.

Date and Signature

Finally, at the very bottom of the document come the date and your signature. Although I don't formalize this sign-off section as an absolute, doctrinal component of all One-Page Proposals, I do think it is important in most cases. This is a formal business document, after all; close it appropriately.

Patrick G. Riley, 15 April 2002

The Sequence Is Sacrosanct

The north-south sequence of sections I have outlined above has an internal logic that I hope you recognize and can appreciate. It follows the basic tenets of the single-sheet proposal idea that Khashoggi shared with me long ago and reflects the addition of a few wrinkles and improvements that I developed over many years of experience. The sections act like stairs, if you will, that are cemented in place one by one to carry your target reader from point A (no knowledge and no interest) to point B (full knowledge and full interest) and to do so quickly. The sequence is the strength; it cannot be deconstructed or rearranged and still retain its persuasive power.

Chapter 5

TRANSLATING YOUR KNOWLEDGE INTO THE ONE-PAGE FORMAT

Step 1: Sort Your Research and Thoughts

Now that you have a basic understanding of each part of a One-Page Proposal and the reasons for its deliberate construction, you can begin shaping your own proposal in your mind. It's human nature to start picking up the pace when you've got a good idea of the road map ahead, but hold on. The best first step is to do a bit of old-fashioned manual organization:

⇨ Gather all your notes, all your research—indeed, everything you've written, photocopied, or even doodled so far—and put each item into one of eight file folders labeled Title, Subtitle, Target, Secondary Targets, Rationale, Financial, Status, and Action.

⇨ Use your new knowledge about the definition and goals of each section to guide you. Don't leave anything out; at this point, practically nothing is irrelevant.

⇨ If you're working primarily onscreen, you can do the same thing—create eight folders on your desktop and sort all your scans, downloads, documents, and other files into the appropriate folder.

For example, if you're like me, your Rationale folder might contain newspaper articles about a company's CEO or an article about the recent firing of the old CEO, a couple of Internet articles and press releases about the completion of a recent project, a recent report of company revenues and earnings, a letter from the CEO describing the company's priorities in the year ahead, and editorial opinion letters from the community in which the company is based. In addition, I would include my most recent bio, descriptions of my last couple of projects, an excerpt from my company's Internet site, and probably a descriptive paragraph about the targeted project.

Step 2: Downsize

Even at this early stage you'll find some material that clearly is not going to be important to keep. Focus on one section at a time, absorb the content, make a few appropriate cuts, and it's time to move on to the next. Trying to hop, skip, and jump randomly through the folders will only cause confusion and make it more difficult to master each section fully and quickly.

Expect the thickest bundle of material to fall into folders three (Target) through seven (Status). Pay no attention to the length or amount of material in those sections right now. Having them in the right folder is enough.

You may have *no* research material in some folders, like Title, Subtitle, or Action. These are not research-based sections, but during this preliminary stage keep a pad of paper close by on which to jot down a list of possible titles, subtitles, and action sentences. Eventually these ideas can be added to the appropriate folders.

Step 3: Prioritize

In each folder, organize your material in sequence from the most important or relevant material to the least. Once you see it arranged this way, you may find it easier to start dispensing with the lesser material—so go ahead—but any stray nugget of usable information should be thrown in with the more important papers. What you're doing, it may soon become clear, is creating a sequence of thought, which should lend itself to a logical sequence during the writing phase. Again, don't worry about the amount of material you have—we'll cut it down later.

This kind of prioritizing will require that you bring value judgments to bear on your material and a certain breadth of knowledge as well. I've found that prioritizing the Rationale folder always presents the greatest challenge, as it usually contains the most material and requires a deft touch to arrange in useful order.

By the time you've finished this process you will have organized all your material, and you will be increasingly comfortable with all the information you have gathered.

Step 4: Start Writing

Now comes the critical conversion—transforming your research material from a stack of sequenced papers into a start-up document containing discrete, stand-alone sentences. Starting with the Target folder (you can skip the Title and Subtitle folders—they are special cases), take a clean sheet of paper and write one sentence for each important piece of information still residing in the folder.

Note: We're not writing the One-Page Proposal yet—this is simply an organizational procedure and a method for getting your first words on paper. Style points don't mean a thing here; just write a basic sentence that summarizes or represents an informational point in your folder. Don't concern yourself with gaps or redundancies; this is meant to be an imperfect process. As rough as it looks, by the end of each folder you will have cobbled together a list of sentences that, if you have prioritized your material correctly, flows to a large degree in logical order.

At this point you may want to step away from what you've written and gain some perspective for the next step: review.

⇨ Is all your pertinent research represented in at least one of the sentences?

⇨ Do the statements follow a logical progression of thought within their sectional domain?

⇨ From folder to folder do they accurately reflect the conclusions and understandings derived from your research?

Assuming they do, let's take these sentences, by folder, and try to assemble them into paragraphs. That is, change your disconnected *list* of sentences into a connected *sequence* of sentences, based on the logic of a normal written paragraph. Do this for each appropriate folder (Rationale, Financial, and Status). For the Title, Subtitle, Target, and Secondary Targets folders, the paragraph form does not apply.

What you should have now is a document that more or less summarizes the results of your research, your financial knowledge, your goals, and your intent. It's not a One-Page Proposal; it's not even the first draft, but it is the starting point for writing one. The document you've just created may be three to four pages in length—and that's fine. The work ahead will involve compressing the data and sharpening the language until you achieve the goal of a single page. You just climbed the steepest hill on our journey; getting this far is a huge accomplishment.

Step 5: Take a Break

Whenever I reach the point when I have a serviceable pre–One-Page Proposal document, I stop, read all my notes one more time, and then pull back and ask myself—

⇨ What am I trying to accomplish?

⇨ Have I captured everything I want to say?

⇨ Is it clear?

⇨ Is anything missing?

⇨ Are there any gaps in my logic?

⇨ Are there any unsupported claims?

⇨ Do the numbers add up?

⇨ And—most important—are the basics of my proposal *persuasive*?

Often, this brief moment of reflection has reoriented my thinking or revealed a new direction. For example, years ago my wife and I decided to buy a beautiful 125-year-old sawmill in the heart of Litchfield County, Connecticut. The mill was spectacularly situated on the East Aspetuck River, but it had been abandoned for fifteen years and was completely dilapidated. Local residents placed bets on when it would fall into the river! The structure, however, was beautiful, and people often stopped to photograph it.

Our purchase created two problems, one economic and one political: the mill would require millions of dollars to renovate; and the property was zoned for an operating sawmill, but the Township of Washington Depot didn't want it to be used for commercial purposes. A restaurant and an office building had already been proposed as a reuse for the building and had been rejected by the town planners.

Enter my wife and I, with a desire to convert the sawmill into a single-family home. We had several strikes against us: we were out-of-towners, we knew we couldn't do it without a tremendous amount of local support, and we knew that every stage of renovating the old mill would be highly scrutinized by the inevitable detractors. To generate community cooperation I started writing a proposal that we could take to city planners, our bankers, our building team, and others whose support we would need to make our vision a reality. When I finished the predraft and was ready to begin writing the One-Page Proposal, I thought I had covered all the bases. As I paused and reviewed, however, I realized that I had included all the facts and figures about the planned construction, but I had failed to communicate a sense of our sincerity and respect for the mill and its history within our new community. This, I felt, was a crucial psychological step, necessary to bridge the gap between "us" and "them."

So I researched the rich history of the mill—who built it, how it was used, where the lumber milled on the site had come from, and even which surviving barns in the county had been constructed of lumber milled on our site. As I wrote my first draft I made sure to add all this information to our One-Page Proposal. When it was finished my wife and I delivered it successfully to a variety of audiences, each of which eventually agreed that we were the proper new caretakers of their landmark building. The Riverdance Mill project was approved, and today it is one of the most beautiful old mills in New England. (See page 96 for the complete One-Page Proposal.)

So, use a short interlude between the organization phase and the writing phase to settle into the proposal you're about to write. Before putting it on paper you should be comfortable and confident in the approach you will take.

Chapter 6

WRITING THE ONE-PAGE PROPOSAL

Title: Headline the Story

As we've seen, the final document always has a title, which is placed at the top of the page in all caps. This is our headline, and it does what a newspaper headline does—tells the reader quickly what the story is about. The title does not have to be a complete sentence; in fact it rarely is. I like to keep my titles only one line wide; a second line detracts from the telegraphic quality and takes up too much space. The type size of the title may vary from 10 to 12 points, depending on the number of words, but the type should always look different from any other type in the proposal. You can accomplish this simply by boldfacing your 12-point capital letters.

The best titles state the subject of the proposal simply. The reader needs to know immediately what your proposal is about, and you should be able to provide as much quite easily. Typical use of this technique might yield titles such as:

⇨ A NEW MUSEUM OF GLASS IN NEW YORK

⇨ AN EMERGENCY FLOOD MANAGEMENT PLAN

⇨ A NEW COMPENSATION AGREEMENT

⇨ REALIGNMENT OF THE AMERICAN LEAGUE

Too simple? Not really. What you want here is a framework both easy to comprehend and memorable. The title is not meant to be descriptive; it is a *label* that communicates the proposal topic. Clever or abstruse titles increase the risk of losing the reader before you've got him hooked.

I've been tempted to be clever in the past. In my One-Page Proposal for Duke Solar, my initial title was "Solar Power Marketeering." My thought was to play on the *eer* letters in marketeering, as e.e.r. is a well-known acronym in the alternative energy business standing for "efficient energy renewables." The pun seemed clever and reflected a subtle point I wanted to make within the proposal. After seeing it in type, however, it seemed too cutesy in the context of a utility company. The culture of utilities is conservative and engineering-driven. In the end I settled on something simple, direct, and conservative: "Duke Solar Strategic Markets Development Project." It worked: the head of Duke Solar kept reading. . . . (See page 97 for the complete One-Page Proposal.)

Subtitle: Build on the Title

The purpose of the subtitle is to further define the topic of the proposal, give it dimension and flavor, pique the reader's curiosity, and provoke him to read on. Like the title, the subtitle does not need to be a complete sentence. It should appear in upper- and lowercase letters, in no more than two typeset lines, just under the title.

Word choice comes into play here. Feel free to be a bit more expressive by using descriptive words and phrases:

➡ *A NEW MUSEUM OF GLASS IN NEW YORK*
A soaring statement in glass and steel to house the priceless Dale Chihouly Collection

➡ *AN EMERGENCY FLOOD MANAGEMENT PLAN*
Critical procedural and training improvements for evacuations

➡ *A NEW COMPENSATION AGREEMENT*
Modernizing an outmoded formula to create fair payment schedules

➡ *REALIGNMENT OF THE AMERICAN LEAGUE*
A strategy to create new geographic rivalries and logical travel schedules

Notice how the subtitle adds a second level of information, thereby clarifying the subject of the proposal, but does so with an evocative flair. The subtitle is not a throwaway line; take some time to craft it so that it plants apt descriptors in the reader's mind (e.g., soaring, priceless, outmoded, critical, new, logical).

Years ago my wife and I created a One-Page Proposal for Sony in which we pitched a series of six low-budget films using Sony's new High-Definition Television (HDTV) technology (see page 98 for the complete One-Page Proposal). Sony was interested in gaining a foothold in the American HDTV market, and my wife was interested in producing feature films. Our One-Page Proposal was designed to catch the attention of Sony's board of directors in Tokyo, in particular its chairman, Akio Morita. My title was simple—"HDTV Feature Films." My first stab at the subtitle was "New Films for New Technologies." On second thought, it didn't sound quite right because I hadn't appealed to the audience and given them a compelling reason to relate to the proposal. Adding the words *Sony* and *to attract U.S. consumers* made all the difference: "New films to attract U.S. consumers to Sony's new HDTV technologies."

Beneath the subtitle is the word *TARGET* in capital letters followed by a colon. The target statement always begins with *To*, as in:

⇨ <u>*TARGET*</u>: To build a glass structure in midtown Manhattan to showcase the finest American glass artists, principally Dale Chihouly.

⇨ <u>*TARGET*</u>: To implement the Corps of Engineers' new flood management master plan to save both lives and property in the lower Mississippi flood plain.

The target statement describes your proposal's intent: what you want to accomplish. Author Stephen Covey calls this "beginning with the end." After all, if you don't know where you want to end, there is a good chance you won't know where to start. If your destination is unclear, you won't be successful in convincing your reader to go with you on the journey the proposal initiates.

I try to keep my target down to one central objective. For example, in the HDTV proposal I used the following: "To establish the market for Japanese High-Definition products in the United States by producing profitable U.S.-made High-Definition feature films."

That's it: one central objective.

If you've done your research, you'll already know something about your reader. Try to use your knowledge of his wants and needs, as I did with Morita above, to nudge him toward taking ownership of the proposal and wanting what *you* want. The best target outlines an outcome both you *and the reader* desire. Sony and my wife and I wanted to establish the market for their HDTV systems in the United States—in their case to sell products; in our case to become the first producers in an important new wave of feature films.

Altogether, the title, subtitle, and target will most likely require no more than twenty seconds of reading time, but in that instant the reader makes what may be his most important decision: whether or not your project interests him enough to read on. The One-Page Proposal format has been clear and up-front about what you want. The reader who continues reading is interested.

Secondary Targets: Clarify Your Goal

Your proposal will have one main objective, which you've just stated as the target. Now you can list additional goals, which I call secondary targets, as a complement to your main objective.

Secondary targets should be expressed in the same manner as the primary target but set off with bullets or other comparable design elements on the left side. This treatment focuses the reader's attention and adds emphasis to each sentence. There may be dozens of secondary goals for your project, but my advice is to list no more than five or six.

These are bullet points, so keep them short and snappy. A secondary target is the logical extension of the main objective and has to make sense in that context. For example, in our imaginary Museum of Glass proposal, our secondary targets might be:

⇨ To provide a permanent home for the Dale Chihouly Collection

⇨ To become the headquarters of the American Art Glass Association

⇨ To provide needed lecture and workshop space for glassworking master classes

⇨ To increase museum tourism in Manhattan

An inappropriate secondary target might be:

⇨ To provide construction opportunities for Teamsters Local 189, which specializes in glass fabrication

This is a potentially worthy goal but out of sync with the other secondary targets and a bit narrow and particular to the interests of one group instead of the city as a whole.

You must be sensitive to the point at which the piling on of secondary targets begins to seem gratuitous. Stop while the list is credible. None of your secondary targets should seem like a stretch to the reader; a good list of secondary targets makes your proposal sound increasingly beneficial and viable. Your reader should be imagining all the wonderful things your project will accomplish; your multifaceted, multidimensional payoffs can sound irresistible.

The rationale is your argument, your "pitch." Drawing on your knowledge and research, write two or three paragraphs of convincing prose that assert your argument. There are traditional stages to a written argument, and they go by different names in different professions. I have my own three-part structure: Setting the Stage, Compelling Points, and The Pitch. Remember, these three parts of the rationale are not literal headings to be set in type but are the three organizing sections of your overall pitch.

Let's build our case in 150 words or so. We'll start with the first subsection of the rationale block: Setting the Stage.

Setting the Stage

Your challenge is to accomplish the following in a few sentences:

⇨ Capture your reader's interest.

⇨ Give the reader a sense of who you are and what you know.

⇨ Summarize the relevant background material and circumstances that propelled the writing of your proposal.

Basically, you want to establish the context of your appeal and explain the situation to which your proposal is responding. In just a few sentences you need to give the reader an understanding of what is at stake so that they can evaluate your claims objectively.

A clear setup is vital for a successful pitch, so be fastidious in your word choice here. Use a positive tone to explain why the target (your objective) is important and necessary, and let the reader buy into your line of reasoning.

One of the best One-Page Proposals in history is the Declaration of Independence, a great example of how important it is to set the stage. Thomas Jefferson wrote the Declaration for two audiences: King George III of England and the people of the thirteen American colonies. To the king he was proposing independence, and to his fellow Americans he was proposing a united battle against the British should the king decline the proposal.

From the start the outcome was uncertain. Anti-British sentiment was by no means universal. It was essential that Jefferson set the stage for his American readers before explaining the rationale for independence. I won't reproduce it all, but here are a few choice sentences from what I would consider Setting the Stage:

> When in the Course of human events, it becomes necessary for one people to dissolve the political bands which have connected them with another, . . . a decent respect to the opinions of mankind requires that they should declare the causes which impel them to the separation.
>
> We hold these truths to be self-evident, that all men are created equal, that they are endowed by their Creator with certain unalienable Rights, that among these are Life, Liberty and the pursuit of Happiness. . . . That whenever any Form of Government becomes destructive of these ends, it is the Right of the People to alter or to abolish it, and to institute new Government. . . . But when a long train of abuses and usurpations . . . evinces a design to reduce them under absolute Despotism, it is their right, it is their duty, to throw off such Government. . . .

It goes without saying that this is one of the most powerful documents ever written. We can admire it on many levels, and one of them is its manifest understanding of how to lay the exquisite groundwork for a winning argument. Jefferson establishes the background that necessitated his proposed idea, and he does so with a building progression that leaves you eagerly awaiting his next step in the plan.

Once you've done similar work, the stage is set for the next step of the rationale block: Compelling Points.

Compelling Points

In the next paragraph, build toward the climax of your argument by piling on persuasive facts. Use the pertinent data from your research to support your assertion that the target and secondary targets will be achieved by executing your proposal. The facts should be irrefutable and timely and should illustrate why your project provides the best solution to the situation at hand. There's no need to be overly emotional or passionate in your language here; the weight of your factual statements should leave the right impression on your reader's mind. Keep building until you reach a sort of prose crescendo, which is the end of your windup—now let's pitch.

The Pitch

Now at last you stride purposefully onto the mound. If your lead-up has been done well, the pitch comes across not as a jarring hard sell but as a logical conclusion. Tell the reader what your proposal, if approved, is going to do. Explain why and how those benefits—the target and subtargets—will be realized.

For example, the Pitch part of the Declaration of Independence perfectly follows the setup of the paragraphs above:

> The history of the present King of Great Britain is a history of repeated injuries and usurpations, all having in direct object the establishment of an absolute Tyranny over these States. To prove this, let Facts be submitted to a candid world.
>
> He has refused his Assent to Laws, the most wholesome and necessary for the public good.

And on and on, listing twenty-seven grievances, a perfect setup for this sentence:

> We, therefore, . . . do . . . solemnly publish and declare, That these United Colonies are, and of Right ought to be Free and Independent States. . . .

In our own century, the same rules apply. In this final section of the rationale, explain to your reader what will happen if your proposal is approved, why you are certain that result will occur, and why he should be the one to approve it, supporting all your claims with as much evidence and logic as you can muster.

Timing Issues—Yours and Theirs

As I write this book, I am in the process of developing a proposal for a new and large philanthropic foundation. The person who runs this foundation was the founder of a major computer-industry company; he has established a foundation dedicated to improving the quality of our lives through education, science, and conservation. So far I have spent a year researching this wonderful foundation. Because it is just now in the process of being formed, the foundation's timing considerations and my own interests are not yet quite in sync, and to push forward prematurely could have a detrimental effect. In other words, I'm ready for them but they aren't ready for me. Ultimately, when the timing is right for both of us, I plan to make a One-Page Proposal they can't refuse.

What timing issues are central to your proposal? Are there deadlines, drop-dead dates, or seasonal considerations that are driving the need for a decision? Is there an event, a meeting, a trade show, or a convention that is critical to your plan?

Rare is the project for which time is in no way an issue, and it is here in the rationale that you include any pressing time concerns.

This is also your chance to impart:

➭ The dates of important events in the project's history

➭ The deadline by which you need the reader's help

These indications of time do not constitute a paragraph unto themselves but should be included in the rationale whenever appropriate.

Financial: Spell Out the Numbers

Every proposal involves either the spending of money, the saving of money, or the making of money—sometimes all three. This section offers an opportunity to show the reader that you are completely familiar with the financial aspects of the proposal and that you are responsible and respectful of money—your own and other people's. The best way to accomplish this is to put yourself in the reader's frame of mind. An investment is both an opportunity and a risk. The reader, I guarantee, will concentrate on the risk. The experienced reader will know the main causes of project failure, many of which are financial—cost overruns, cost surprises, collapse of financing, uninsured losses, increased pricing, and poor financial oversight and management. Could any of these causes impact your proposal? Here's where you do your best to demonstrate that you've anticipated the pitfalls and made allowances for them.

Perhaps your proposal has no financial implications at all. For example, say you're proposing a change in an office procedure, a plan for the neighborhood Christmas party, or a parking plan for a new manufacturing plant. If there is no money component, this section is where you explain why there are no costs or expenses, hidden or otherwise.

What if your proposal concerns an improvement to a manufacturing process that will cost nothing but may save your company thousands of dollars? This is the place to quantify the cost savings, using broad strokes and gross numbers. You may have to do a more thorough financial report later, but by then your proposal will have done its job—it's all over but the details.

Whether you're providing financial details simply for information and context or asking directly for financial help, it's best to make this finance paragraph brief, accurate, and easy to understand. This is not an annual report. Hit the highlights, using big-picture, important numbers only. You don't even have to write this in paragraph form; an itemized list can work just as well.

To illustrate the importance of this section and how to do it for yourself, let me use an acutely personal example. My wife, Roberta, is a film producer with experience at all levels of television and movie production. She started as a location manager for the TV series *Streets of San Francisco*, then became an independent location manager for big-budget studio films. She developed San Francisco Studios, the first major film studio in our area, where movies like *Star Trek 4*, *Innerspace*, and the TV series *Midnight Caller* were shot. In 1989 she decided to become an executive producer, an occupation that involves developing a story from scratch, hiring a writer, putting together the production team, and finding the money to make and distribute the film. In the process she had to demonstrate to some very savvy people in the motion picture industry her knowledge of the intricacies of feature-film financing and had to enumerate the valuable relationships she could bring to bear on the film's prospects for success. To accomplish this she developed a One-Page Proposal entitled "Are You Lonesome Tonight" (see page 99 for the complete One-Page Proposal).

FINANCIAL: The film is budgeted to cost $2,800,000 and expected to generate revenues to the producers of $5,929,000 over a seven-year period, representing a profit of $3,341,000. The breakdown is as follows:

Estimated Budgeted Costs: Above the Line $999,000, Below the Line $1,496,000, Other $306,000

Estimated Producers' Distribution Revenue:

Domestic Theatrical	$4,928,000
Foreign Theatrical	1,228,000
Worldwide Video	1,620,000
Pay TV	1,120,000
Network and Foreign TV	373,000
Other Adjusted Costs	(3,341,000)
Total	_$5,929,000_

The designated production company, Bandai Entertainment Group (USA), a joint venture between Pacific American Corporation and Bandai Co. Ltd., is considering two options to produce the film: (1) to put up the production money directly and arrange for distribution through Columbia, in which case they would benefit directly from the film distribution revenues estimated above, or (2) to arrange for a "negative pickup" with a distributor like Columbia with a one-time fee to the producers of approximately 175 percent of the negative budget costs (i.e., for _Are You Lonesome_ approximately $4,900,000).

In an industry in which even low-budget film production costs start in the millions and inexperienced producers do little but pitch the contents of the film and leave the details to others, Roberta's comprehensive approach was refreshing. She went the distance with her one-pager, describing her targets and backing them up with information on the expertise and reliability of her production team, the important costs and benefits of shooting and editing the film from her own studio, and names, dates, and details.

Look carefully at the financial section of Roberta's proposal. Financial viability is addressed right at the beginning through clear statements of cost, projected revenues, and—most important to a major film distributor—anticipated profits. It takes only one discrete sentence for her to outline her production costs, demonstrating a familiarity with the intricacies of production "above" and "below" the line (Hollywood parlance for differentiating creative talent from workers). She aligns her primary target (audiences who like "psychological thrillers . . . in the tradition of _Fatal Attraction, The Accused, Klute,_ and _Play Misty for Me_") with her projected revenue numbers by spreading the distribution revenues across all sources and then cleverly backs in the negative cost of production to reaffirm the budget figures in her first sentence. She also reveals a very pertinent relationship between Bandai Entertainment Group and Columbia Pictures that could materially improve the odds of success.

Are You Lonesome Tonight, starring Jane Seymour, was successfully released in 1991 with wide distribution to theaters in Europe. To this day Roberta still gets royalty checks.

A word of caution: Resist all temptation to "sweeten" the financial facts. They are what they are. In this section you must express yourself honestly, competently, and confidently. These traits are often important enough to carry a deal forward despite less-than-ideal economic conditions or even serious financial demands.

Status: Where the Deal Stands Now

In this section you tell the reader what elements of your proposal are in place and which are still in limbo.

⇨ Do you have some money commitments already? What are they? How much are they? Are they conditional?

⇨ Do you have support of a nonfinancial nature? From whom?

⇨ Is there a roadblock in the proposal's way—a person, a company, or a government agency?

⇨ Are any contracts signed, grant-of-rights given or pledged?

⇨ Are any key agreements held up by red tape or attorney review?

It is best to fully disclose all these details here in the status section. Be frank, and don't ignore the negative or the controversial. Explain exactly where the deal stands now. If someone has turned down your proposal already, say so. Your reader may know it anyway, and most businesspeople are not deterred from good ideas by prior rejections. In fact, investors often look for turnarounds, the opportunity to create success from projects others have spurned (especially if the other is a business competitor).

The status section gives the reader a current picture of your deal and, most important, a sense of your enthusiasm. One persuasive way to prime the pump is to show some early success or positive results. If you can demonstrate momentum from others in addition to your own enthusiasm, highlight it. Positive movement prior to investment is a crucial factor for moneylenders and important supporters.

The status paragraph also acts as a setup for the action paragraph that follows it. You're finally about to ask for something, so this is the windup before your final pitch. If, for example, the whole deal is in place, awaiting only the last bit of financing, what better time to say it than right before you ask for the financing. If the deal is brand-new and has no support yet, say so, but say it in a way that will encourage the reader to become the first one in.

Action: If You Don't Ask for Something, It's Not a Proposal

So far, your One-Page Proposal has provided the reader with who, what, when, and where. The action sentence now tells the reader how—as in how he can help you. Don't assume the reader will necessarily have deduced his role in your plan simply by reading the previous parts of the One-Page Proposal. Spell it out here in your action statement: Do you want to borrow money from him? Do you want him to join a committee? Do you want his backing? Ask, and ask unambiguously, explaining exactly what you want.

By this point you should be able to make your "ask" sentence precise and clear. Investors don't want a request that they sense is being spun. It simply wastes their time.

One of my mother's good friends was Murph Couzins Slattery, a philanthropist and grand dame of Detroit. Murph's pet project was Detroit's Children's Hospital, to which she contributed much of her own wealth. She did not like to ask her friends for contributions, but when the hospital found itself in need of capital improvements, she let her friend and neighbor Sebastion Spering Kresge (founder of Kmart) know that she wanted to speak to him concerning the situation. When Murph arrived at Kresge's home he was rushing to a Detroit Tigers baseball game, already decked out in team jacket and cap. He had fifteen minutes before he had to leave and, after listening to her plea, explicitly asked Murph how he could help her with the hospital. She was ready for the question. She said she wanted him to contribute enough money to build a teaching auditorium at the hospital, where doctors from all over the world could assemble to discuss pediatric breakthroughs. "How much do you need?" he asked. She replied, "Ten million." He agreed on the spot, then left for the ball game.

As this story illustrates, important people appreciate knowing specifically how they can be of help. If Murph had not thought through the amount and purpose of the gift she was soliciting, her meeting would have been a lot less productive—or possibly even a lost cause.

Also, make sure that what you ask for is doable. You shouldn't ask for something the reader cannot provide. Your research should have provided you with an idea of what your reader can do. Ask for something clearly within his or her capabilities.

Date It and Sign It

The date is important because it shows that the information provided in your One-Page Proposal is current right down to the day. The signature symbolizes personal commitment and conviction. It took a lot of courage for the fifty-six men who signed the Declaration of Independence to put their names in writing. If the colonies had lost the war, they all would have swung on the gallows. The One-Page Proposal is a personal transaction; your name, reputation, and good character are behind it.

Occasionally I add a copyright designation at the bottom as well. I do this when the information I have used in the One-Page Proposal is sensitive or confidential and I want to protect it from being disseminated or published freely. Using a copyright mark does not guarantee privacy, but it does put the reader on notice that the material is for the reader's eyes only and should be distributed further only with the consent of the author. For ultrasensitive material, you might consider placing the word *Confidential* at the top or bottom of the page.

Ready to Write?

So there's the playbook for your One-Page Proposal. I hope I have given you a good idea of how to put the pieces together in the right order. Now all you have to do is write it. Don't be intimidated! All your research and preparation, combined with the step-by-step plan I just gave you, should make it simple and even enjoyable to write your One-Page Proposal. You don't have to be a professional writer or any sort of genius to create a persuasive document; just draw on what you know, and follow the One-Page Proposal blueprint.

I've given you a follow-the-bouncing-ball approach, and I'm not disparaging my technique by saying so. I find great comfort in knowing that I don't have to be ultracreative every time I propose something. If I had to write like William F. Buckley and invent a new form every time I had an idea to pass along, I would never get the proposal off my desk. Instead, I spend most of my time learning the details and background of my topic and actually very little time on the writing itself. Why? Because I take it step by step, writing each section from top to bottom in basically one sitting. Once I have all the details in hand, the first draft of my One-Page Proposal takes me about two hours.

Chapter 7

IMPROVING, REDUCING, AND COMPRESSING

Congratulations. You're the proud owner of a first draft. Now it's time to revise it and make it shine. Two things might still need correcting—length and wording. Sit back and read it straight through as if you were the intended reader. Don't stop to take notes. Then read it a second time and start making revisions based on the following factors.

Length

There is only one thing to do if your proposal is still longer than one typed page: Begin cutting. You *must* get it down to one page. What gets eliminated first? Here are some suggestions:

Eliminate Interesting but Unnecessary Facts

You've gathered a lot of facts and data, but all of it may not be necessary to carry the pitch. You may have included some information because you found it interesting, unusual, or startling, or perhaps because it was a great find in your general research. Take your red pen and strike through the sentences that are not absolutely critical to the comprehension or persuasiveness of the core idea of your proposal.

For example, you're proposing to bring a Broadway show to your city, and in your Rationale section you write, "This show was written by David Mamet and was originally produced by David Merrick at the Regency Theater on 42nd Street in Manhattan in 1985." Interesting facts if you have plenty of room. But if you're looking to save space, you can certainly eliminate everything after "David Merrick." Where and when the show was first mounted are only tangentially pertinent to a decision involving whether to risk money on a theater venture.

Eliminate Redundant Information

You're proposing to build a new office building in your city. Your title is "THE SMITH CENTER OFFICE COMPLEX." Your subtitle is "Anchored by the tallest, most modern office building in downtown Smithville." Later in the rationale you state, "The new Smith Center will be the highest and most cutting-edge office building in the downtown area, with 44 floors of state-of-the-art features. . . ." And still later, in the Financial block: "Since it will be the tallest and most modern building in downtown Smithville, it will be a magnet for new business in Smith County, qualifying it for both county bonds and tax relief from the city."

We get the "tallest, most modern" angle—three times. It's an important aspect of the proposal, but it doesn't need to be repeated, especially if you're pressed for space.

Eliminate the Obvious

We cautioned you earlier to remember that sometimes your target reader knows a great deal about the industry or topic your proposal concerns. Perhaps that's why you chose her as your target reader in the first place. When your reader possesses all the knowledge she needs to judge your proposal, take out those sentences that are inappropriate for her. There's no need to remind Armand Hammer of the profit potential of the oil business or to explain film distribution to George Lucas. Include only the details that are unique and proprietary to your proposal. Review your proposal through your reader's eyes—is there anything that might make her think, "No kidding, bub?" Basically, take out anything that would make *you* seem naive for including it.

Once you're done cutting content, you can start cutting to improve your style.

The English language changes all the time, for reasons of history, context, technology, and our speedy cultural flux. Writing in English offers both a challenge and an opportunity—there are so many words to handle and so many *senses* of those words. Our language offers gifted writers a virtually unlimited toolbox for expressive, subtle, and stylish writing. That said, in general my feeling is that style should always take a backseat to simplicity, directness, and clarity in creating a One-Page Proposal. A One-Page Proposal isn't the place for linguistic flights of fancy. You've got to make your case, support it, and ask for something in a concise and unmistakable fashion.

Here are a few language usage tips to help cut your proposal down to size:

Eliminate Wordiness

For example: "Building near the water has its advantages. The first advantage to be considered is the economy of building near the water." [21 words] This could easily become "Building near the water offers construction economies. . . ." [7 words]

Instead of "A successful building will enhance its site and will fit naturally into its site" [14 words], how about "A successful building will enhance and fit naturally into its site" [11 words].

Instead of "The reason why we all need this product is that . . ." [10 words], how about "We all need this product because . . ." [6 words].

Instead of "A new addition will be built on the side of the structure, and this addition will be developed into a computer room" [22 words], how about "A new addition will be built and will become a computer room" [12 words].

Eliminate Adjectives, Adverbs, and Other Descriptive Language

Most adverbs and intensifiers take up a lot of room without adding a lot of content. Consider:

⇨ "We must admit that the old method was ~~staggeringly~~ popular." (*Popular* is a strong enough word to carry your meaning.)

⇨ "The garden will become a~~n extraordinarily~~ beautiful place, with thousands of ~~amazing~~ red roses." (Both *extraordinarily* and *amazing* are unnecessary.)

Eliminate Excessive Detail

Avoid the temptation to wax poetic. You are offering a business proposition, not penning a novel. Consider:

⇨ "The passenger ship, seaworthy many years ago but now needing a complete overhaul, was moved to storage, ~~as is so often true of things that should be discarded.~~" (Does your proposal need your editorial observation about the instinct to save what is no longer useful?)

⇨ "Twenty years ago, if you had lived on Oak Street, only a small portion of which remains today, you could find a barber, a butcher, a grocery store, a pharmacist, a police station, and a fire station, all within four blocks of your house." (Evocative, but we can handle this thought in a few words: "Twenty years ago all the necessary stores and services were within walking distance of Oak Street.")

Eliminate Tautologies

There are a number of commonly used business phrases that may sound perfectly reasonable but are either incorrect, wordy, or can be scaled down. Consider the following improvements:

⇨ "What's wrong with modern business ~~of today~~ is . . ."

⇨ "Let me repeat ~~again~~ the point I made earlier . . ."

⇨ "The passengers will ascend ~~up~~ the stairs . . ."

⇨ "We all foster the idea ~~in our own minds~~ that . . ."

Careful word choice is a great way to reduce word count. The key is precision: choosing the noun, verb, or adjective that *exactly* expresses your thoughts helps you communicate not only well but efficiently. One word will often do where you might have used several, cutting right to the meaning you desire. Chances are, your potential business investor is not looking for the next Tolstoy but for the next Bill Gates, so save yourself the extra room and keep it simple!

Wording

Even if the length is okay, on rereading you may feel that the wording of your proposal needs improvement. Think about the following as you try to buff your One-Page Proposal to a high shine.

Use the Third Person

The One-Page Proposal is not a résumé. Its success should not hinge upon a personal appeal, but rather upon the value of the business proposition itself. To keep your voice from becoming that of a sideshow pitchman, be sure to write the entire proposal in third person. Use *he, she,* and *the Company* as opposed to *you, me,* and *us.* This will prevent the reader from feeling as though he has received a piece of direct-mail marketing. This point is especially salient when dealing with certain foreign investors, who often take a culturally less individualistic approach to business transactions.

Express a Positive Attitude with Positive Words

Writing persuasively demands clarity and coherence, but it also requires words and phrases that add emphasis. Make an effort to use strong, active words instead of weak, passive ones. Negative sentence constructions and attitudes will impart weakness to your proposal. You can see it in this sentence: "We cannot reach our fund-raising goal if Starlight foundation does not contribute something. . . ." To your reader (and potential investor), that sounds defeatist and a little offensive. Write it positively: "Starlight foundation's generous contribution will be a vital addition to the donor group and will enable it to fund the charity's most important work." Putting a positive spin on the sentence will tend to create a positive reaction in your reader.

Here's another example of poor word choice: "The need for this facility seems obvious, but so far no one has seen the need or felt the urgency to get this project moving. Your firm is among the last two or three companies that can help." How is that supposed to make your reader feel? Like the only fool who hasn't yet turned you down? You can express your urgency in a positive way, without seeming desperate: "Despite a clear demonstration of need, other worthy causes have currently captured the lion's share of local charitable giving. Starlight foundation's leadership and prescience can be the springboard to reversal of that trend and start a new round of generous donations."

Avoid the Oversell Trap

You are trying to persuade your reader to take the action you desire. Try to convince by the logic and benefits of your proposal rather than by using "sell" words. Your temptation is to sell and sell hard because you care about your proposal, but don't fall into the trap of empty advertisement.

Look over your proposal and see if you've used superlatives without support:

⇨ "The best washing machine ever designed"

⇨ "The most effective automotive radar system ever built"

⇨ "The most desirable cookware set ever offered to the American public"

Using phrases like that is an easy way to arouse your reader's suspicions. If you can support your claim, great. But if not, back off and describe your idea in more credible terms.

Remember, getting your reader to back your proposal is an act of trust. You won't be trusted if you sound like a con artist.

Check Your Grammar

The old strict rules of grammar have loosened up over the last twenty years or so, and I won't say that's a bad thing. Modern writing can be very effective when it breaks free of old boundaries and reflects instead the freshness of contemporary speech. But by and large the One-Page Proposal is a traditional business document, and the basic rules of grammar always apply. Even if you're not a professional editor you can probably spot many basic errors if you read carefully and self-critically.

One classic mistake to watch out for is lack of subject-verb agreement. In other words, every verb has to agree in number with its subject. Is there agreement in the following example?

➡ *"The wings of an airplane enables it to fly."*
Enables may sound right to your ear because of its proximity to a singular noun—*airplane*—but the subject of the sentence is *wings,* and therefore the plural verb form, *enable,* is correct.

Or in this example:

➡ *"General Electric, along with Microsoft and Intel, were participants in the lawsuit. . . ."*
Even though there seem to be three subjects, there is only one—General Electric—and the verb should be *was.* Better yet, rewrite the sentence: "General Electric was a participant in the lawsuit, as were Microsoft and Intel."

The trick is to determine whether your subject is singular or plural, despite all the parenthetical phrases, and make your verb conform.

Check Your Spelling

Spelling errors can include both typos and accidental misspellings of proper names, uncommon words, or esoteric industry terms. Some consider these mistakes incidental, but don't kid yourself: they can be quite damaging. They create an impression of sloppy, inaccurate work and betray the credibility and thoroughness that may otherwise exist in your proposal.

Dozens of words are commonly misspelled in business communication. Often these errors stem from the tendency to spell by ear. Common mistakes involve using a word that sounds right but has a meaning other than the one intended. For example, be conscious of the following words, which are very commonly confused:

affect and *effect*—affect = to influence; effect = to bring to pass

capital and *capitol*—capital = a financial resource; capitol = a building in which a state legislastive body meets

council and *counsel*—council = a legislative body; counsel = advice, usually legal

it's and *its*—it's = contraction of *it is* (as in "it's cold outside"); its = possessive form of *it* (as in "its only drawback")

lead and *led*—The past tense of the verb *lead* drops the *a* (as in "I will *lead* the group tonight, but yesterday Mary *led* it")

principal and *principle*—principal = chief or primary; principle = a fundamental truth or governing law of conduct

stationery and *stationary*—stationery = paper and envelopes; stationary = not moving

there, their, and *they're*—there = at that place (as in "over there"); their = possessive of *they* (as in "to their advantage"); they're = contraction of *they are* (as in "they're on board")

to and *too*—When you mean *also*, add an extra *o*.

weather and *whether*—weather = the state of the atmosphere; whether = if

who's and *whose*—who's = contraction of *who is* (as in "Who's there?"); whose = possessive form of *who* (as in "Whose is it?")

Other common words are misspelled simply because they are difficult to spell, such as: *accommodate, apparent, commitment, foresee, forty, judgment, morale,* and *occurred.* The spell-check software in your word processor can help you here, but do not rely on it totally. It will not catch misspellings that constitute another word (e.g., *read* for *red; scene* for *seen*).

Misspelling proper names and company names is especially dangerous. For example, I once saw a movie proposal that cited "my good friend John Houston." Ouch—it's Huston. The proposal writer was trying to imply a close relationship with the legendary director, but the mistake just made him look like an outsider. Likewise, spelling a company name incorrectly highlights your unfamiliarity with the subject or the industry. People might pronounce the name of the well-known pharmaceutical giant F-i-z-e-r, but it's spelled Pfizer, and the computer giant Cisco has no doubt tired of being confused with the food company Sysco. Double-check all proper names and company names for accuracy.

Punctuation

This can be a complicated business, even for a seasoned editor. My advice is to simplify your sentence structure so you don't risk losing the reader to a complex, poorly punctuated sentence. To be sure your commas, colons, and semicolons are in the right places, refer to *The Associated Press Stylebook* or *The Chicago Manual of Style.*

Abbreviations

Use only the most common, acceptable abbreviations, such as Inc., Mr., and St. or generic acronyms such as NFL, CEO, or NATO. When in doubt, spell it out.

Capitalization

There is a high probability that there will be proper names and subjects within the One-Page Proposal, so consult your style manual to guide you in capitalizing words like *president, vice president, ambassador,* and other forms of address such as *Sir, Madam, Dr.,* and so on.

Contractions

Normal business-writing standards should be the norm in creating your One-Page Proposal, and in most instances it's best to avoid using contractions in business correspondence—they create an inappropriately familiar tone.

Helpful Books

There are many books that can be helpful to authors in all matters of writing style. Here are a few.

⇨ *The Elements of Style* (William Strunk Jr. and E. B. White)—a classic text that has served writers for generations

⇨ *A Dictionary of Modern English Usage* (H. W. Fowler)

⇨ *A Dictionary of Modern American Usage* (Bryan A. Garner)

⇨ *The Careful Writer* (Theodore M. Bernstein)

⇨ The Modern Language Association's *Line by Line* (Claire Kehrwald Cook)

⇨ *Merriam Webster's Collegiate Dictionary* (be sure to get the latest edition)

A serviceable writing style is a useful skill no matter what your profession. Usually it's the result of clear thinking and a basic grasp of grammar and usage rather than vocabulary. As I've said before, you don't need a bevy of ten-dollar words to write a successful One-Page Proposal. You just have to find a simple, clear voice. When you use simple words with certainty, you'll give your reader the impression of fluency and competence, and those are powerful, persuasive qualities for your One-Page Proposal.

Once completed, the One-Page Proposal should ideally be a fixed document, to be modified only when:

⇨ Your project's financial details change

⇨ Your project's status changes

⇨ Certain sections need to be tailored to fit specific readers

It's important to keep the language of the One-Page Proposal free of references or images that the average reader won't understand so that you don't find yourself constantly having to rewrite for new investors. The readers of your One-Page Proposal may vary widely in education, background, native language, and national origin, so be wary of using Americanisms. An analogy to cavalry strategy in the Civil War might mean nothing to an Asian investor. Likewise, use of current American slang will fall on deaf ears in most business contexts. Resist the temptation to be hip, trendy, or showy.

Chapter 8

A GREAT ONE-PAGE PROPOSAL

We can review the principles behind the One-Page Proposal until we've mastered every theory, but the best way to write a successful one-pager is to start by studying an example of a polished one. In this case, our model is based on my speculation regarding one of the great engineering projects in history—the construction of the great pyramid erected to the pharaoh Cheops almost five thousand years ago. Following the principles of the One-Page Proposal, I've created a document that the pharaoh's chief architect might have used to pitch his idea to the great ruler himself.

Imagine that you are Hemon, an architect to the great Pharaoh Cheops. You have been designing structures in honor of the pharaoh for years, but now you want to create the ultimate tribute—a potential source of both widespread acclaim and substantial reward. This is the chance to leave your mark, to extend your skills beyond minor remodeling jobs, and to distinguish yourself from the gaggle of royal sycophants.

And so you conceive a new design for the pharaoh's eternal resting place: a pyramid with four sides, rising to an apex 482 feet above the desert floor, an imposing structure that will memorialize the great ruler throughout history. Confident that your design is genius, now your goal is to persuade Cheops himself to appoint you Chief of Works and authorize the financing and construction of the project.

You are aware that you've set yourself a serious challenge. Cheops is a formidable character with a big ego and a jealous entourage. Though you happen to be his cousin—a status that may win you some favor—you also know that the pharaoh is surrounded by a battery of master builders, surveyors, rock quarry owners, slave union bosses, and lawyers, each of whom has an agenda and turf to protect. They are going to be reviewing your idea, too, so you know you must craft your One-Page Proposal with care and forethought to appeal to as varied an audience as possible.

Title and Subtitle

The title needs to be memorable but simple—shoot for five or six words. Your first attempt: "Pharaoh's Burial Place." But that's not quite right—it's too pedestrian. "An Edifice for All Time" also won't do—it's creative but vague. Then you hit on the perfect mix, simple yet dramatic: THE GREAT PYRAMID OF CHEOPS.

The pharaoh knows what a pyramid is, but he needs to be intrigued. So you amplify your meaning in the subtitle: *A powerful monument in tribute to Pharaoh, in an ageless geometric design.* It's a subtitle designed to pique the pharaoh's curiosity and appeal to his sensibilities—in this case, to his ego. The words *powerful* and *ageless* play to Pharaoh's towering self-regard. Here, in the context of a memorial tribute, the flattery is entirely appropriate.

Target

Here is where you must consider what the pharaoh truly desires and then find a way to offer it. Given that the ruler is twenty-six years old and possesses every luxury imaginable, what can your monument offer that's new and exciting? Immortality. This pyramid unites the pharaoh and Egypt for all eternity. Your target reinforces Pharaoh's own goals: *To build a monument honoring the greatness of Egypt and ensuring the eternal life of Pharaoh.*

If you have properly identified the pharaoh's desires, your proposal will succeed all the more readily by promising to satisfy them. Notice that the language never mentions that *I* or *we* wish to prevail upon Pharaoh but simply proposes to build the monument. Self-promotion might offend Pharaoh or his bureaucratic cronies. Keeping the language impersonal keeps the focus on the work at hand.

Secondary Targets

You have learned through research and experience that Cheops is a major proponent of technological innovation and also tends to give a lot of weight to his wife's opinions. You translate that information directly into a pair of secondary targets:

⇨ To demonstrate Egypt's cutting-edge technologies
⇨ To provide an eternal resting place for the queen

Rationale

In this particular project, there is only one crucial timing factor, and you lead off your rationale section by demonstrating your awareness of it: *The great Pharaoh Cheops has decreed his intention to build a monument* during his lifetime *that reflects his greatness and that of Egypt.*

Now you set the stage for your pitch by giving the background information: *Ever since the Great Unifier, King Narmer, was buried at Abydos in a pit tomb topped by a moundlike superstructure, the pharaoh of Egypt has been assigned a unique status in the eyes of men and the gods. Yet none of the previous tombs has reflected the ultimate relationship between the sun god Ra and the pharaoh himself. Nor has the architecture of these structures been advanced enough to protect the pharaoh's body and his treasures as they travel through to the next life. Already evidence of grave-robbing can be seen at the monument for Pharaoh's father, King Snefru.*

The stage is now set for the central pitch. The pharaoh needs to know you can do the work, and you need to convince him. Be as authoritative as you can: *Hemon, a most innovative architect of Pharaoh's royal palace, has developed a novel and superlative design for such a monument in the shape of a great pyramid. The proposed design is unique in the history of Egypt but promises great continuity with the design of existing structures and the traditions of our land. Hemon has an outstanding record of handling large projects in Pharaoh's palace. A trusted member of Pharaoh's family, he is a manager whose competence is unchallenged.*

Now you summarize with five or six compelling points that emphasize the achievement of the objectives stated in the target and secondary targets: *Expected benefits of the proposed work include: (1) a magnificent site for the pyramid on the strongest bedrock of the Giza Plain; (2) the monument's projected status as the largest structure in the world; (3) a design that aligns the pyramid with the stars on a north-south axis, perfectly orienting Pharaoh to the setting and rising sun; (4) advanced methods of protection against grave-robbing, guaranteeing Pharaoh and his queen safe passage into the next world; (5) engineering within a maximum deviation tolerance of less than eight inches for the entire structure; and (6) a facing of Tura limestone, which has the highest reflective qualities of any stone in the world.*

Financial

The pharaoh Cheops is a divine king and retains sole control over all the wealth of Egypt. Still, even he has financial constraints, and as a savvy guardian of his wealth he is bound to have concerns about a project of this scale. Can the task be accomplished within feasible financial limits? Will his management team work with you to control expenses? Can the pyramid be completed comfortably in his lifetime? And what about engineering questions: Will this revolutionary design work? Will the bedrock of the proposed site support the structure's weight and yet still be close enough to the Nile to ensure the convenient transportation of stone?

Your investigation has convinced you that it can be done and at an acceptable cost. The project will require the marshaling of much of the pharaoh's resources, but it is manageable. In an effort to be completely straightforward you write: *As the largest monument of its type in the known world, the Great Pyramid will require one-fourth of the treasury of Egypt to complete—an increase of only 5 percent over that spent by Pharaoh's father, after taking into account the growing tax base on the grain harvest from Semna West to the Delta. From preliminary drawings, Pharaoh's royal palace engineers estimate that the 482-foot pyramid design will require approximately 2.3 million blocks of stone, each weighing 2.6 tons. The cost of construction can be paid out gradually over 23 years—the time it will take to complete.*

Status

Here you let the pharaoh know how much work you have done already and what parts of the deal are already in motion. Remember, your goal is to answer each question before the pharaoh has a chance to ask it: *Preliminary drawings are complete. Quarries near Giza have pledged to meet the demand for both limestone and granite. New sources of gold and cedar wood for ramps have been located in Egypt's new territories in Byblos and Lower Nubia. The Department of Civil Service can provide a workforce of 100,000 craftsmen and workers to work during the flood seasons, which will ensure completion by 2528.*

Action

You have known from the beginning what you want Cheops to do, but as candid as you've been, you can't assume that he will deduce it from the proposal. State your needs explicitly: *For the great Pharaoh Cheops to appoint Hemon as his Chief of Works, specifically authorizing him to carry out the building of the Great Pyramid.*

At least that's how I'd like to think Hemon would have done it. As practice, why not try writing One-Page Proposals for other major projects in history—the Panama Canal, the Hoover Dam, the Roman Colosseum, the Great Wall of China. A quick trip to an encyclopedia, or the Internet, will be all the research you need, and it will serve as a fun way to familiarize yourself with One-Page Proposal construction.

THE GREAT PYRAMID OF CHEOPS

A powerful monument in tribute to Pharaoh, in an ageless geometric design

TARGET: TO DESIGN A MONUMENT HONORING THE GREATNESS OF EGYPT AND ENSURING THE ETERNAL LIFE OF THE PHARAOH

- To demonstrate Egypt's cutting-edge technologies.

- To provide an eternal resting place for the queen.

The great Pharaoh Cheops has decreed his intention to build a monument during his lifetime that reflects his greatness and that of Egypt. Ever since the Great Unifier, King Narmer, was buried at Abydos in a pit tomb topped by a moundlike superstructure, the pharaoh of Egypt has been assigned a unique status in the eyes of men and the gods. Yet none of the previous tombs has reflected the ultimate relationship between the sun god Ra and the pharaoh himself. Nor has the architecture of these structures been advanced enough to protect the pharaoh's body and his treasures as they travel through to the next life. Already evidence of grave-robbing can be seen at the monument for Pharaoh's father, King Snefru.

Hemon, a most innovative architect of Pharaoh's royal palace, has developed a novel and superlative design for a monument in the shape of a great pyramid. The proposed design is unique in the history of Egypt but promises great continuity with the design of existing structures and the traditions of our land. Hemon has an outstanding record of handling large projects in Pharaoh's palace. A trusted member of Pharaoh's family, he is a manager whose competence is unchallenged.

Expected benefits of the proposed work include: (1) a magnificent site for the pyramid on the strongest bedrock of the Giza Plain; (2) the monument's projected status as the largest structure in the world; (3) a design that aligns the pyramid with the stars on a north-south axis, perfectly orienting Pharaoh to the setting and rising sun; (4) advanced methods of protection against grave-robbing, guaranteeing Pharaoh and his queen safe passage into the next world; (5) engineering within a maximum deviation tolerance of less than eight inches for the entire structure; and (6) a facing of Tura limestone, which has the highest reflective qualities of any stone in the world.

FINANCIAL: As the largest monument of its type in the known world, the Great Pyramid will require one-fourth of the treasury of Egypt to complete—an increase of only 5 percent over that spent by Pharaoh's father, after taking into account the growing tax base on the grain harvest from Semna West to the Delta. From preliminary drawings, Pharaoh's royal palace engineers estimate that the 482-foot pyramid design will require approximately 2.3 million blocks of stone, each stone weighing 2.6 tons. The cost of construction can be paid out gradually over 23 years—the time it will take to complete.

STATUS: Preliminary drawings are complete. Quarries near Giza have pledged to meet the demand for both limestone and granite. New sources of gold and cedar wood for ramps have been located in Egypt's new territories in Byblos and Lower Nubia. The Department of Civil Service can provide a workforce of 100,000 craftsmen and workers to work during the flood seasons, which will ensure completion by 2528.

ACTION: For the great Pharaoh Cheops to appoint Hemon as his Chief of Works, specifically authorizing him to carry out the building of the Great Pyramid.

Hemon

The Khashoggi Proposal That Should Have Been

I wrote earlier about my meeting with Adnan Khashoggi and how his advice and counsel spurred my interest in and development of the One-Page Proposal concept. If I had known then what I know now, I would have proposed my deal to Khashoggi in a different way. I would have prepared a sharp, crisp, One-Page Proposal that laid out all the important details, gave him a quick understanding of the commitment I was after, persuaded him of the project's value, and indicated exactly what I wanted him to do. Let's look at the document I should have written for Khashoggi.

EQUIPPING THE U.S. MILITARY IN THE RED SEA, INDIAN OCEAN, PERSIAN GULF

A joint American-Saudi venture of General Resources Corporation and Triad

__TARGET:__   To win a large developing market by supplying materials and strategic services to the United States military's Rapid Deployment Forces at their bases in Somalia, Djibouti, Kenya, Egypt, and Oman

In response to the fall of the shah of Iran and the Soviet invasion of Afghanistan, in 1980 United States president Jimmy Carter announced the formation of the Rapid Deployment Force (RDF) in order to defend U.S. interests in the Persian Gulf. The RDF is based at Diego Garcia, an island located in the heart of the Indian Ocean, however, it is commanded from MacDill Airforce Base in Florida. To compensate for Diego Garcia's distance from the United States, the U.S. military signed three agreements that provided for the use of certain facilities in strategic locations for positioning of troops and equipment: Oman (Masirah Island and Muscat), Kenya (Mombasa), Somalia (Berbera), Djibouti, and Egypt (Ras Banas).

Triad, a company owned by the Khashoggi family of Riyadh, Saudi Arabia, has engaged in significant business in Oman, Kenya, Egypt, and to a lesser extent Somalia and is well positioned to support certain RDF initiatives. Additionally Triad has a unique understanding of Saudi and American regional military interests dating back to 1953.

In 1980, in direct response to the emerging RDF market and certain "buy American" constraints imposed by the U.S. Congress, Pat Riley (BA University of California at Santa Cruz, MA Oxford) and his brother Tom Riley (BS Stanford, MBA Harvard) used their experience in the region and their knowledge of industrial equipment to establish General Resources Corporation (GRC). Through GRC, the brothers negotiated exclusive deals with large U.S. nonmilitary equipment companies (Dresser Industries, Gardner Denver, Bucyrus-Erie, John Deere). In addition, they established in-country facility support with leading families in Somalia, Djibouti, and to a lesser extent Kenya. Finally, GRC has established relationships with the appropriate federal equipment purchasers in Washington, D.C., and related contacts with the appropriate foreign ambassadors in Washington, D.C.

GRC is proposing a 50/50 joint venture, for which it will provide the work, and Triad will provide the working capital.

__FINANCIAL:__   An estimated $10 million is required over a two-year period to exploit the market fully. The proceeds will be used entirely for marketing and winning contracts related to RDF. GRC projects gross earnings of $50 million. The FY 1985 Department of Defense budget allocates $59 billion for the RDF, "of which about $47 billion is for the Persian Gulf." A Congressional Budget Office report stated that "the RDF, and particularly the plans for a larger version, could give rise to pressure for eventual increases in the defense budget" ("Congressional Budget Office, Rapid Deployment Forces: Policy and Budgetary Implications," Washington, D.C., February 1983, p. xiii). The initial military assistance intended to finance the construction of the pre-positioning bases is $700 million. The follow-on budgets are being presented and are expected to be substantial.

__STATUS:__   GRC has set up the entire strategic development plan and is ready to implement.

__ACTION:__   Adnan Khashoggi to meet with Pat Riley to decide whether to proceed and finalize the agreement parameters if going forward.

Patrick G. Riley, 15 April 2002

Chapter 9

PRODUCTION VALUES

Now that you've perfected the content of your One-Page Proposal, it's time to produce the finished item. The proposal is not just a collection of ideas, it's also a physical entity, and as such it's a demonstration of your standards of quality. You don't have to spend a fortune etching it in marble or glass, but an attractive final product can make a real difference in the proposal's success.

Paper

Your One-Page Proposal is a personal emissary from you to the reader. For this reason, every element of your proposal should bespeak quality. Even if you intend at some point to transmit your One-Page Proposal by other means, such as fax or e-mail (which we will cover in the next chapter), you should always produce a superb hard copy for direct or follow-up presentation.

⇨ Start with a good quality cotton-fiber paper, at least 24 pounds in weight, of standard size (8½ by 11 inches in the United States).

⇨ Do not use your personal stationery or business letterhead—use a blank sheet of paper. White paper is always good, and certain buff or gray hues do just as well.

⇨ Avoid brightly colored paper with exaggerated watermarks or ornamentation; it looks unprofessional and will tend to distract attention from the proposal's content.

Typeface and Type Size

Readability is of utmost importance, so pick a standard business typeface such as Times Roman or Baskerville, in a 10- to 12-point font. Draw attention to section headings by using slightly larger type or boldface. Don't be tempted to use 8- or 9-point type as a way to squeeze more material onto your page—that's just too small for easy readability, and your proposal will likely end up in the recycling bin. Fancy decorative typefaces for the title or subheads can easily become distracting and look unprofessional, so be sure to keep it simple.

The best approach is to single-space the proposal, with a line space between paragraphs and sections. For shorter proposals 1½ spaces between lines can work. The title should be centered or set flush left and should be set in the largest point size on the page.

General Appearance

Always use black ink to print the One-Page Proposal. Your copier may have color capability, but colors can be distracting and can reduce clarity, so stick to basic black. Use a good laser printer; dot-matrix printers produce poor letter quality, even on the best setting. If you don't have a laser printer, go to Kinko's or another service bureau and have them print it for you. A crisp, professionally printed document is essential to making the right impression.

Use generous margins on all sides, starting with one inch on the top, bottom, left, and right. If you need more room, decrease the dimensions by a quarter inch until everything fits. Note: the margins should never be less than a half inch all the way around.

My One-Page Proposals are always flush left, ragged right, like a standard business letter. There's no problem with using justified text (flush left *and* right), as long as the technique doesn't produce odd word spacing or unusual hyphenations. If you prefer the orderly look of justified text but find you're having these problems, try a smaller font size, or adjust the justification settings in your word-processing software accordingly.

One effect that can crop up during formatting is the hyphenation of the last word in a line, which can look sloppy. Usually the ragged-right format eliminates them, but some software will hyphenate a long word that falls at the end of a line of text. You can usually override such hyphenation manually, but if that creates a funny-looking short line, it might be best to reword rather than let the hyphenation stand.

Chapter 10

PRESENTING THE ONE-PAGE PROPOSAL

Marilyn vos Savant, the writer and columnist listed in the *Guinness Book of World Records* as having the world's highest IQ, was asked in her column in *Parade Magazine:* "Which is greater, the spoken word or the written word?" She answered: "The written word, by far. It's of better quality, having benefited from planning, organization, and revision; it has greater stability, making our memories look ephemeral by comparison; and it can reach more people over the course of time, including those not even born yet." The same might be said of the advantages of the One-Page Proposal over the verbal pitch so common in today's business and professional world. The printed One-Page Proposal ensures that your pitch is delivered with all the forethought, care, professionalism, and polish that the process allows. You gain complete control over the presentation of your argument.

Having said that, what's the best way to get your One-Page Proposal into the hands of your target reader without it seeming like an anonymous piece of paper? You may have gained time for thoughtful preparation, but you don't want to lose the advantages of personal contact.

The One-Page Proposal should never be sent without an introductory conversation with your intended reader, either in person or by telephone. If you want the proposal to be read and taken seriously, then there's no substitute for the personal connection of a one-on-one conversation.

For best results you should have a face-to-face meeting with the reader where you can orally review the proposition and leave the hard-copy One-Page Proposal for his perusal. If that is not possible, discuss the proposition with your intended reader by telephone, and follow that conversation with the overnight delivery of your One-Page Proposal. I send my proposals unfolded, flat, in 9 by 12-inch mailing envelopes or in one of the overnight envelopes UPS or FedEx provides.

E-mail attachments and faxes are fine, but only as intermediates—they should never be relied on as a substitute for the hard copy. If you use one of the intermediates as your initial delivery method, always follow up as soon as possible with a paper version, even if the intended receiver has not yet expressed interest.

Telephone Protocol

In paving the way to present your One-Page Proposal, you might find yourself following one of several courses of action:

1. If your contact says, "Sure, I'd love to meet": Set up a meeting time and go to the appointment armed with the One-Page Proposal, which you can present during or immediately after the meeting. Bring several copies, just as you would a résumé.

2. If your contact asks you specifically, "What would you like to talk about?": Don't try to answer that question fully over the phone; you don't want to risk trying to ad-lib your way through a too-hasty pitch. Instead, read him your target sentence and tell him you've prepared a One-Page Proposal that covers all the key issues, a copy of which you will send over in preparation for an in-person meeting. Send him a copy of your One-Page Proposal with a short note confirming the appointment time, reminding him of your conversation, and reaffirming your personal interest in meeting with him.

3. If your contact says, "I'm not sure I can help. Why don't you send me something in writing first? If it looks good we can set a time and get together": Send over your One-Page Proposal with an attached note affirming your respect for his opinion and the value of his time. Indicate that you will call in three days to set up an appointment.

The fourth option, of course, is that the person turns you down over the phone. "No, not interested. Thanks, but no thanks." Take heart, you certainly aren't the first person with a good idea to face rejection. George Lucas got turned down by almost every major studio in Hollywood when he first pitched *Star Wars*. If your first-choice reader turns you down, don't give up completely. Write him a thank-you note in which you reiterate your respect and regret at his decision—and attach a copy of your One-Page Proposal. Express your willingness to meet at another time to discuss the project should his feelings change. Finally, pick yourself up and redirect your One-Page Proposal to another promising person—an associate, a competitor, whomever. Adjust the proposal to suit the new reader, if necessary, and make a new round of calls. You're still on track.

Know Your Proposal Inside and Out

The great Hollywood movie producer and pitchman Robert Kosberg says there are four basic principles guiding a good in-person pitch:

⇨ Be certain your idea is pitchable.

⇨ Rehearse your pitch until you know it cold.

⇨ Show your passion.

⇨ Visualize your success in advance.

Kosberg's advice is sound: When you're going in for that all-important in-person meeting, it's crucial that *you* believe your idea is sound and will be a success. Writing the One-Page Proposal is an exercise with room for trial and error, but pitching the proposal *in person* is a much more unpredictable process. Depending on the circumstances, you might have to start by talking about the financial aspects. Or you might find yourself having to start by responding to a specific question about your project's status. No matter what, the best advice is to know your proposal well enough that you could pitch it anywhere—at 1 A.M. aboard a yacht, for example, as I did with Adnan Khashoggi. You should be prepared to deliver a crisp, energetic pitch in person in even the most unusual circumstances. I have presented one-pagers in military bivouacs, at power lunches in Hollywood, around a kitchen table, during walks on the beach, over a short-wave radio, via the Internet, in a bank board room, and in geisha houses in Japan. I've pitched them in jeans, suits, safari gear—even once in my pajamas! When you know each section of your proposition by heart, you'll be quick and ready when the time comes, whatever the circumstances.

Kosberg has another theory that has become a mantra for the Hollywood elite: If you can't explain your proposal in one sentence, either your idea is bad or you don't know it well enough. Hollywood producers have always made instant judgments about film ideas based on "log lines" prepared by their story analysts. Here's an actual one from film history: "The former lover of a cynical World War II casino owner arrives in Nazi-occupied Morocco accompanied by her husband whose heroism forces the hero to choose between his cynicism, his still-strong feeling for his ex-lover, and his latent patriotism."

We all know instantly which movie this describes—*Casablanca*.

You have to know your proposal so well that you could explain it in one sentence if you had to. In a way, you've done that already—in the target line of your One-Page Proposal. Always keep the target in mind when you're asked, "What's this proposal all about?"

We live at a time of terrific innovation, not just in the creation of new companies but within the walls of our greatest existing companies as well. The success of America's businesses depends on innovation from within.

According to a saying attributed to Ralph Waldo Emerson, who lived more than one hundred years ago: "If a man can write a better book, preach a better sermon, or make a better mousetrap than his neighbor, tho' he build his house in the woods, the world will make a beaten path to his door." Paraphrased for the twenty-first century: Though you may be in your organization's lowest echelon, if you put forward a compelling proposal, the powers that be will beat a path to your cubicle.

The best companies (big or small) know this, and today more of them are building their businesses on this principle. On the other hand, sometimes internal innovation can be thwarted by the system itself—especially in older, larger, or more conservative companies.

This needn't be so.

If you're running a company or managing a division, the One-Page Proposal is an excellent tool with which to empower your employees. Once they have a clear format with which to express themselves, you'll be amazed at the innovations that can come from your subordinates. A One-Page format for ideas can make a substantial difference to your performance as a leader and the company's performance as a whole.

If you're a salaried employee with a bright idea, the One-Page Proposal is a great way to push forward that proposition and make a tremendous difference to your company, your supervisor, and your own career.

The efficient nature of the One-Page Proposal facilitates the flow of ideas in a business environment. If one assumes it would take an individual three to four months to write a sixty-page proposal and another two months for the proposition to percolate through the organization (perhaps requiring ten people in the chain of command to spend six hours each digesting the proposal), then in such an organization the maximum production of innovative proposals would be two per year.

If, on the other hand, one assumes that people in a company have adopted the One-Page Proposal as a standard means of circulating new ideas, and it takes a maximum of one month to write a One-Page Proposal and as little as five hours for ten people to evaluate it, that increases the production of innovative proposals to twelve per year—a 600 percent increase in productivity, saving tens of thousands of dollars in man-hours alone.

If you're an employee of a company that has not adopted the One-Page Proposal as a standard means of communicating innovation, adopt it for yourself and use it freely within the company. Your superiors will catch on, and you and your ideas will get noticed. If you're a leader of such a company, consider making the One-Page Proposal standard operating procedure. You'll be amazed at the innovative ideas locked inside your own people—ideas that can drive your profitability in the years ahead.

Put Your Heart into It

You probably won't have to travel twelve thousand miles to make your proposal, as I did with Don Hunt and William Holden, but you will have to travel the distance between your idea and a face-to-face meeting to make the idea a reality. The great news is that the proposal takes you more than 75 percent of the way there.

What will take you the other 25 percent of the way is your passion, which is just as important as page length. The key to your success with the One-Page Proposal, beyond the obvious value of your idea, will be the personal commitment you have to your project—commitment that will be reflected in both your proposal and your in-person delivery.

In his famous book *The Power of Positive Thinking*, Norman Vincent Peale recounts a story about a famous trapeze artist who was instructing his students on the secrets of the high trapeze bar. One of his best pupils, faced with the prospect of actually giving it a go, froze. "I just can't do it," he said. The coach understood. He put his arm around the student's shoulders and told him the secret that would release him from his fear. His advice was simple: "Throw your heart over the bar, and your body will follow."

One purpose of presenting the One-Page Proposal is to allow the reader to say no if she's not inclined to pursue your idea or for some reason cannot do what you ask.

No isn't necessarily a bad outcome; in fact, it could be good for both you and the reader. If your reader's no reflects the truth as she sees it and expresses her honest disinclination to do what you ask, that's fine. Your courteous acceptance of her decision will enable you and the reader to part friends and maintain a good relationship. By giving her an opportunity to review your well-thought-out proposal, you may even improve your personal relationship and keep the door open for future ideas. And she might even give you a referral to a colleague who, in her opinion, would be a better fit for your project.

No isn't the worst answer you can receive; maybe can be worse. With no you can move in any new direction. With maybe you are left hanging in limbo, unsure whether the proposal was unpersuasive, the deal itself was uninteresting, or your reader was just having a bad day. A maybe tempts you to sit around and hope for a yes. I treat a maybe as a no. Waiting stalls the process, makes you anxious, and takes the wind out of your sails. I say give her a few days to decide, then call her. If she says no, move on. If she isn't available or won't take your call, move on. You are looking for a person who wants to take action. A maybe person will never get you where you want to go.

Many years ago, under the strangest circumstances, in a remote village in Ethiopia, East Africa, I spent two days with Craig Claiborne, the famed food columnist and author of *The New York Times Cookbook*. We met at a dirt airfield, both of us having been bumped off a DC-3 that was to take us to Addis Ababa. The next plane would not arrive for two days. There was nothing to do but get acquainted, but it seemed we had nothing in common. He was an expert in great foods and wines, and at that time I was a "bring-'em-back-alive" animal trapper in nearby Somalia. But over the next few days we began to share stories and experiences as we relaxed on the veranda of our small hotel. He described his youth in Mississippi and his long journey to the dining tables of royalty. Through his stories he was able to convey the full gamut of his experience with food, from haute cuisine at Chez Denis in Paris to his favorite deli in New York City. His passion for food and life was contagious, enough so that when I finally got back to civilization the next year I bought his cookbook—the first and only cookbook I have ever read.

What struck me about the book was that the instructions were simple and easy to follow, whether they involved preparations for everyday meals or elaborate dinner parties. Claiborne assumed a certain amount of confidence in the reader, and the result was a style that was neither arrogant nor condescending.

That is the impression I hope this book will have made on you. If you follow the spirit of its recommendations, I have confidence that you'll be able to use the One-Page Proposal to make your dreams come true.

Chances are, one of the reasons you bought this book was to make a difference in your life—to go beyond your current circumstances, to make an ambitious venture happen, to convert an idea into a proposition and the proposition into a reality. In effect, you might be trying to break out of one phase of your life and into another. One of the side effects of using the One-Page Proposal is that it enables you and the people around you to see your true self.

Take the example of Chester Carlson, a young patent lawyer who filed repetitious forms for his employer until he came up with an idea for a technology that would "do the world some good and also . . . do myself some good." At first alone and then with a partner he developed a new "dry-copying" duplicating machine that would solve the problem of monotonous reproduction of patent documents. It took over twenty presentations before he interested a company in codeveloping his invention.

The company that eventually made the first sale of his copier has since been renamed Xerox.

The One-Page Proposal is a communication tool specifically designed to get your ideas into the mind of another person in a world overwhelmed with words and information. It should provide a fast and effective way to help your ideas become realities.

You have my best wishes for your success.

The One-Page Proposal Support Network

When I finished the first draft of this book, many people suggested that future readers might be interested in receiving direct coaching in One-Page Proposal writing, or even in submitting their proposals for critique and/or improvement. To support that idea, I have established the One-Page Proposal Support Network, which offers a wide range of choice and access to high-quality, responsive technical help.

The One-Page Proposal Support Network offers priority telephone and Internet access to our support engineers. In the United States, call 415-921-8849, or visit www.onepageproposal.com.

We are also coming out with new products to support the One-Page Proposal. Watch for a CD-ROM version to be released soon. In the meantime we are offering our initial users discounts on related products. If you would like to receive additional products or information, please visit our website.

Corporations interested in setting up training sessions for their people on site should also contact us at www.onepageproposal.com.

Appendix

Sample Proposals

SHUTTLE ENTERPRISE EXHIBIT

A special exhibition of the space shuttle Enterprise *in Tokyo, Japan, in 1993*

TARGET: TO DEMONSTRATE TO THE PEOPLE OF JAPAN AND THEIR NEIGHBORS THE UNIQUE CONTRIBUTIONS THE U.S. SPACE PROGRAM MAKES TO MANKIND

- To enlarge Japan's sense of shared responsibilities for the global issues revealed by the space program.

- To convey goodwill and invite opportunities for future cooperation in space between the United States and Japan.

In 1991 Nippon Television Network Corporation ("NTV" or "Sponsor") in cooperation with Japan's Imperial Family, the Prime Minister's Office, the Japanese Ministries of Foreign Affairs and Education, the National Science Museum, and the Science and Technology Agency proposed to sponsor an exhibition of U.S. space technology in Tokyo featuring the space shuttle *Enterprise*. (The *Enterprise* is a dummy shuttle which was used by NASA solely to be dropped from a 747 at high altitude to test shuttle design capabilities for flight.) The Tokyo exhibition was to take place in 1993, and the proposal was made to the National Air and Space Museum ("NASM") of the Smithsonian Institution.

NTV, the largest private TV network in Japan (they recently singlehandedly paid for the restoration of the Sistine Chapel in Rome), has provided for all logistical aspects (transportation and handling, insurance, security, curatorial oversight, and exhibition design). NTV has arranged a team of experts that includes former NASM, Smithsonian, and NASA officials to handle each aspect of logistics for the exhibition. In addition, NTV plans to support the exhibition with its vast media resources (e.g., with regular articles in its two daily newspapers, reaching a combined daily audience of ten million readers).

FINANCIAL: There will be no costs to the United States. The Sponsor and other cooperating Japanese companies and Japanese government agencies will pay all costs associated with the exhibition, including costs incurred by NASM, the Smithsonian Institution, NASA, and the U.S. Navy for staff time as billed. The exhibition is an entirely nonprofit undertaking; all net proceeds will be donated to NASM and the Smithsonian. NTV has made the following financial commitments:

Minimum guarantee on exhibition net proceeds	$2,000,000
Restoration of the spaceship *Enterprise*	750,000
Expansion of NASM's Garber restoration facility	700,000
Broadcast credit for airing of Smithsonian programs	5,000,000
Estimated shuttle transportation costs	9,000,000
Total financial benefit to United States	*$17,450,000*

As part of the proposal, NTV has also agreed to arrange for an "exchange of exhibitions" of similar technological merit (i.e., to provide the Smithsonian with a model of Japan's newest MAGLEV train for exhibition on the mall in Washington, D.C.)

STATUS: The space shuttle *Enterprise* is currently stored in a hangar at Dulles Airport. No longer needed by NASA for testing, the *Enterprise* has been decommissioned since 1984. There are no plans to restore the *Enterprise* to put it on public display in the foreseeable future. The *Enterprise* was last on exhibit at the Paris Air Show in 1983 and at the 1984 New Orleans World's Fair. The written proposal from NTV, dated April 5, 1991, was personally presented to Dr. Martin Harwitt, Director of the Air and Space Museum, on April 11. Some concern has been voiced as to the viability of this project by the subcommittee of the U.S. Congress chaired by representative Sid Yates (D-Ill).

ACTION: Senator Daniel Patrick Moynihan to use his power as a Regent of the Smithsonian and congressional leader to endorse the project for carrying out the exhibition.

THE MILL OF NEW PRESTON, CONNECTICUT

Its Restoration and Conversion into a Residence

TARGET: TO RESTORE AND CONVERT THE MILL OF NEW PRESTON VILLAGE INTO A PREMIERE SINGLE-FAMILY RESIDENCE

In 1875, Oscar Beeman, a local master builder, built a sawmill and carpentry shop on the East Aspetuck River just south of Lake Waramaug. The structure itself was built on the foundations of an old iron ore blast furnace built in 1834—the iron ore having been brought from Ore Hill in South Kent. The mill was powered by the East Aspetuck River, which runs at a rate of 3,000 gallons per minute. Mr. Beeman was a barn builder and used the lumber he milled to build barns throughout northwestern Connecticut—some of which can still be found in the surrounding area, noticeable for their distinctive cupolas, the Oscar Beeman trademark also found atop the mill itself. In their book, *Early American Mills,* published in 1973, Martha and Murray Zimiles said of the New Preston Village mill that it "is one of the most beautiful mills that remains in all the Northeast."

In 1941 the mill was sold to Robert Woodruff, who kept it operational until 1964 and lived in the mill through the 1980s. In 1987 the Woodruff family sold the mill with 5.09 acres of land to Peter Mullen, who neither made improvements to the mill nor occupied it.

On December 30, 1996, Mr. and Mrs. Patrick Riley purchased the mill and the 5.09 acres both as a part-time family residence and as a renovation project, while their two children, Maximilian (16) and Joanna (14), are attending Canterbury and Kent schools—both in the graduating class of 2000. The Rileys' main residence is in San Francisco, California, and they have a beachhouse on the Pacific Ocean in Marin County. The Rileys call the mill *Riverdance Mill.*

Through a design of "spartan elegance," the Rileys intend to make the structure sound, complete the essential utilities, and choose residential improvements harmonious with the mill's existing architecture and the land around it, and to conform to the rules of Washington township.

FINANCIAL: The Rileys paid $▮▮▮▮▮ in cash for the mill. Their approach to the property is as an investment. Their approach to the renovation is to add market value that exceeds their investment.

Preliminary estimates of the renovation costs from six different contractors range from $▮▮▮▮ to $▮▮▮▮, including a low head hydroelectrical power plant using the water to power the building. The costs break down roughly as 72 percent for structural improvements; 15 percent for mechanical (wells, septic, and electrical); and 13 percent for the low head hydroelectrical power plant.

The Rileys' banking relationships in San Francisco are with Wells Fargo Bank and First Republic Bank.

STATUS: Mrs. Roberta Riley will be in Connecticut to spearhead the renovation of the mill at the end of March. On January 31, Mrs. Riley met there with various parties associated with the project. The new number for the mill in New Preston is ▮▮▮▮▮▮▮, although the answering service is not yet operational. Generally the Rileys can be reached through their residence or office in San Francisco. While in Connecticut, Mr. and Mrs. Riley stay with friends in Bethlehem, where they can be reached by telephone and by fax. Brian Neff has been engaged to engineer the project. The homeowner's policy is bound with the Chubb Group through the offices of Spencer Houldin. Flood insurance has been secured. Legal representation is handled by Linc Cornell, Esq., in Washington Depot. Following an evaluation of the banks best suited to their needs for renovating the mill, the Rileys decided to apply for financing through the National Iron Mortgage Company.

ACTION: While in Connecticut Mrs. Riley would like to meet with interested banks to discuss arrangements for a construction/first mortgage loan to support the renovation of the mill.

DUKE SOLAR STRATEGIC MARKETS DEVELOPMENT PROJECT

A sequence of strategic initiatives to drive Duke Solar's core business into the most profitable world markets

TARGET: TO MAXIMIZE DUKE SOLAR'S SHORT-TERM AND LONG-TERM REVENUES AND PROFITS.

1. To wrap DS's global strategy into a high-level presentation for Duke Energy (and prospective strategic partners).

2. To engage Marubeni and examine all Marubeni's ties that could materially affect DS's profitability.

3. To valuate existing alliances (e.g., Energia Hidroelectrica de Navarra) and pending alliances.

4. To identify other alliances that if executed would provide DS with a significant competitive advantage.

5. To act on new market conditions in California's "un-unbundling" of power generation, transmission, and distribution.

6. To track and be prepared to act on corresponding or counterintuitive responses in Nevada and Arizona.

7. To influence President Bush's energy teams (e.g., the Energy Policy Development Group).

8. To seek out unsolicited proposals with DOE's Office of Energy Efficiency and Renewables.

Reliable power is a cornerstone for economic development and advancement worldwide. Electric power is a $215 billion industry. The events of the summer of 2001 as they affected the western United States combined with recent terrorist attacks on the World Trade Center and the Pentagon have accelerated changes in the dynamic power market, *including renewables*. Increasingly: (1) electric power will be a market-driven industry; (2) innovation (products and services) will be required to gain competitive advantage and market share in all deregulated environments; (3) massive capitalization will be required; (4) cost efficiency will become paramount; (5) pricing differentiation will become increasingly necessary to compete effectively; (6) new technologies must be utilized; (7) state-of-the-art information technologies will be required; and (8) corporate cultures will need to reenergize.

Duke as a whole is well positioned to exploit post–9/11 markets, having already refocused on providing BTUs from diverse power plants that they own and operate all over the United States. Duke Solar Energy, LLC, is also well positioned. It has expanded beyond initial goals "to design, market, manufacture, install, and maintain a patented solar system capable of producing hot water, steam, or electricity for residential, industrial, institutional, commercial, and utility customers" and expanded its mission to provide BTUs from renewable energy sources from plants they own and operate (or build for others) all over the world. DS is dedicated to becoming a world leader in renewable energy, by leveraging their solar thermal technologies to combine with others in order to produce BTUs from renewables. Key to Duke Solar's ongoing strategy is the generation of BTUs from renewables and the marketing of those BTUs and associated emission credits to the most profitable markets worldwide.

Patrick G. Riley, a friend of Duke since 1997 when he began working in conjunction with DE&S on offshore power projects, has offered to spearhead the Duke Solar Strategic Market Development Project in order to ensure its goals of expansion are met.

FINANCIAL: Riley has agreed to work on a technical services contract within the range of Duke Solar's budgets for such services.

STATUS: Riley is prepared to start immediately. In 2001 he has met and formed a constructive relationship with the Duke Solar team. John Myles has set sixty days as the first deadline for outcomes from Riley. Riley has agreed to dedicate himself to completing the desired outcomes within that period. Riley has provided Myles with a sample agreement detailing the conditions of the work.

ACTION: John Myles to review the scope of work proposed and credentials of Riley to determine whether to engage Riley to assist as indicated.

HDTV FEATURE FILMS

New films to attract U.S. consumers to Sony's new HDTV technologies

<u>TARGET:</u> TO ESTABLISH THE MARKET FOR JAPANESE HIGH-DEFINITION PRODUCTS IN THE UNITED STATES BY PRODUCING PROFITABLE U.S.-MADE HIGH-DEFINITION FEATURE FILMS

- To produce a package of feature films for U.S. audiences using state-of-the-art Japanese HD technology.

- To establish a prototypical showcase film studio utilizing HD technologies in all aspects of production and display.

- To train and develop a core group of feature cinematographers in HD technologies.

- To exploit the superior high-tech video workforce of the San Francisco Bay Area (vs. film-based Los Angeles).

- To extend HD product range into theatrical laser projection systems.

Japan is the leading developer of High-Definition Video Systems ("HDVS"). In the United States, Japanese manufacturers of HDVS are trying to persuade home consumers to replace their TVs with HDTVs and movie and television producers to shoot their movies using HDVS cameras, editing systems, and display technologies. In particular, Sony (in conjunction with Japan's largest broadcaster, NHK) has identified three areas of HDVS technology for development in the United States: (1) production, (2) transmission, and (3) display.

Pacific American Corporation, at San Francisco Studios, has developed a group of six feature films referred to collectively as the Graffiti Series. The Graffiti Series consists of highly stylized entertainment with strong musical content and special effects expressly developed to be shot, edited, transmitted, and displayed using HD technologies. Pacific American producers believe that because of the stylistic nature of the Graffiti Series, if the films were released hand-in-glove with HDVS in the United States, a substantial leap in market share for Sony could be achieved by providing consumers with a showcase for HD technology. The premise of Pacific American's proposition is that the market for HD is not technology-driven but consumer-driven.

<u>FINANCIAL:</u> The total capital required to develop the Graffiti Series is $7 million plus a contribution of the necessary HD cameras, editing hardware, and related technological support. A breakdown of the film budgets and proposed release dates:

Black Fury	$850,000	1988
Lady Day	1,700,000	1988
Bed and Sofa	900,000	1989
1000 Cranes	1,700,000	1989
Chimera	900,000	1989
The Mystic	950,000	1990

In return for providing the production capital and hardware, Pacific American Corporation will assign to Sony exclusive rights to distribution of the Graffiti Series in Japan in all media (theatrical, consumer video, broadcast TV, music, and other merchandising) as well as worldwide rights to use the Graffiti Series in HD product demonstrations.

<u>STATUS:</u> The Graffiti Series is ready for production: scripts written, budgets made, all creative talent assigned, and facility support at San Francisco Studios agreed. Pacific American is seeking an introduction at the appropriate level within Sony management to begin discussions.

<u>ACTION:</u> The Japanese Consul General of San Francisco, Mr. Ochi, to use his power to arrange a first meeting with Pacific American and Sony and to personally make the face-to-face introductions.

ARE YOU LONESOME TONIGHT

Production: PROD 111

TARGET: TO PRODUCE A FEATURE FILM, OF THE THRILLER/SUSPENSE GENRE, WITH STRONG AUDIENCE APPEAL, AND TO MAXIMIZE ITS RETURN ON INVESTMENT

- To exploit the product vacuum resulting from the screenwriters' strike

- To focus on the topical and highly commercial subject matter of telephone sex

Are You Lonesome Tonight is a psychological thriller written in the tradition of *Fatal Attraction, The Accused, Klute,* and *Play Misty for Me.* The story is set in San Francisco and centers on the phenomenon of telephone sex. The format is nonpornographic, and the film is expected to receive a rating of "R." The producers are Roberta Smith Riley (formerly on the production team for *Streets of San Francisco* and now head of San Francisco Studios) and Paul Pompian (a successful producer of five previous hit movies). The screenplay is written by Wesley Moore (past credit: *Telegraph Hill*). The producers are in discussion with Harry Falk as the possible director (past credits: *Centennial, Hear No Evil,* and numerous other suspense thrillers).

The compelling point of the production is that because of factors within the control of the producers, the film can be made with high production values at low cost. Namely: San Francisco Studios controls both sets and on-location film services, as well as production and postproduction facilities; the veteran San Francisco Studios team has had extensive experience working together shooting feature films in San Francisco on budget.

FINANCIAL: The film is budgeted to cost $2,800,000 and expected to generate revenues to the producers of $5,929,000 over a seven-year period, representing a profit of $3,341,000. The breakdown is as follows:

Estimated Budgeted Costs: Above the Line $999,000, Below the Line $1,496,000, Other $306,000

Estimated Producers' Distribution Revenue:

Domestic Theatrical	$4,928,000
Foreign Theatrical	1,228,000
Worldwide Video	1,620,000
Pay TV	1,120,000
Network and Foreign TV	373,000
Other Adjusted Costs	(3,341,000)
Total	*$5,929,000*

The designated production company, Bandai Entertainment Group (USA), a joint venture between Pacific American Corporation and Bandai Co. Ltd., is considering two options to produce the film: (1) to put up the production money directly and arrange for distribution through Columbia, in which case they would benefit directly from the film distribution revenues estimated above, or (2) to arrange for a "negative pickup" with a distributor like Columbia with a one-time fee to the producers of approximately 175 percent of the negative budget costs (i.e., for *Are You Lonesome* approximately $4,900,000).

STATUS: The script is written. Discussions are proceeding with Columbia Pictures to determine the level of interest and the best options open to the producers. Preproduction is in progress. It is estimated that principal photography will start in the spring of 1989 and require a 30-week shooting schedule. No contractual commitment will be made to the director or other creative talent until the production and distribution arrangements are finalized. The president of Bandai Entertainment Group (USA), Patrick Riley, has submitted the final script and production budgets along with his recommendation to produce *Are You Lonesome* to his counterpart at Bandai Co. Ltd., President Makoto Yamashina, in Tokyo, for his consideration. Under the terms of the 50/50 joint venture, both partners must agree before a picture is selected for production by the company.

ACTION: Mr. Makoto Yamashina to elect whether or not to produce *Are You Lonesome Tonight.*

THE ONE-PAGE PROPOSAL BOOK

A systematic description of the technology of writing a One-Page Proposal that can change the world

<u>TARGET:</u> TO PUBLISH A POWERFUL BESTSELLING BOOK ABOUT THE SECRETS OF USING THE ONE-PAGE PROPOSAL TO ACHIEVE SUCCESS

- To be the only and best book of its kind

- To develop a high-profile, marketable product that provides a high return on investment

- To reach markets that cross industry segments, lifestyles, and cultural lines

- To translate the product and distribute it for revenue in foreign markets

- To provide a platform for evolutionary derivatives (i.e., CD/ROM version)

- To capitalize on the three-year Library of Congress exhibit of famous one-page documents

In 1983 Patrick Riley learned from one of the wealthiest men in the world that a paradigm of successful international business was the ability to write a One-Page Proposal. Acting on this knowledge, Riley and his wife, Roberta, have built their company, Pacific American Corporation, into a widely respected and highly successful San Francisco firm with projects and clients worldwide. The inspiration for the book came not only from their own phenomenal success with the One-Page Proposal, but from a systematic study of some of the greatest One-Page Proposals of all time: the Declaration of Independence, the Magna Carta, the Gettysburg Address, the Bill of Rights, the Mayflower Compact, and the Arecibo interstellar message.

The intended book is a how-to manual complete with

- A guided step-by-step illustration of how to formulate a One-Page Proposal using a hypothetical business scenario.

- Tech support.

- Real-life examples from Riley's career and personal life with applications in business, science, the arts, and family.

The writing method described complements the speed and efficiency of present-day business practice by (a) leapfrogging complex desktop publishing software, (b) creating a user-friendly format for foreign investors, (c) bypassing frustrating information overload, and (d) reducing decision-making time.

<u>FINANCIAL:</u> The key financial objective is market performance in all media. The market positioning sought is between high performers: *The One Minute Manager* and *The 7 Habits of Highly Effective People*. Retail price between $12.00 and $20.00 with large, workbook-type dimensions.

<u>STATUS:</u> The initial draft of *The One-Page Proposal* was completed in February 1997 and revised in 1998. David Bullen, a notable book designer, completed the draft text proof in February 1999 and designed a cover based on a David Hockney painting. Riley has completed a thorough analysis of the market success of various titles in the personal development, leadership, and finance categories and concluded that finding an excellent publisher—one with the skill and experience to launch a first-time author and successfully place this book in the very competitive business books sector—was crucial to success. On June 3, Riley contacted Judith Regan at Regan Books who Riley believes has the power, experience, and track record to make the book a success.

<u>ACTION:</u> For Judith Regan to review the manuscript of *The One-Page Proposal* and decide on her level of interest.